Speak

for

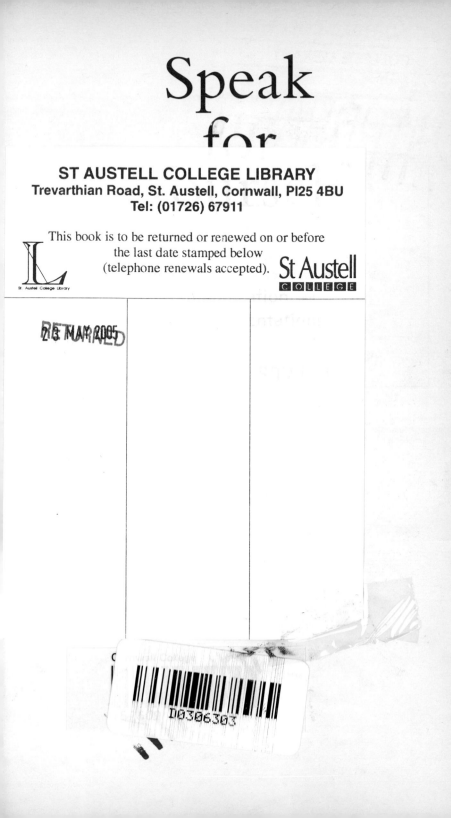

For John's son

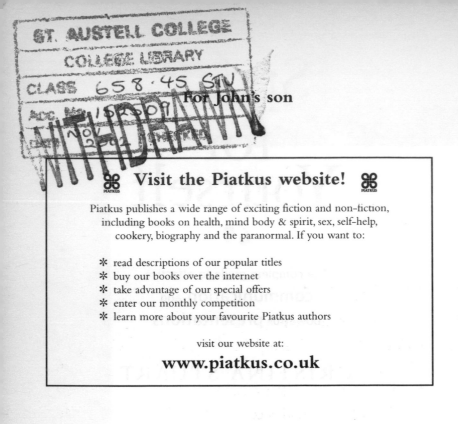

Visit the Piatkus website!

Piatkus publishes a wide range of exciting fiction and non-fiction,
including books on health, mind body & spirit, sex, self-help,
cookery, biography and the paranormal. If you want to:

* read descriptions of our popular titles
* buy our books over the internet
* take advantage of our special offers
* enter our monthly competition
* learn more about your favourite Piatkus authors

visit our website at:

www.piatkus.co.uk

© 2000 Cristina Stuart

First published in 2000 by
Judy Piatkus (Publishers) Ltd
5 Windmill Street
London W1T 2JA
e-mail: info@piatkus.co.uk

This paperback edition first published in 2001

The moral rights of the author have been asserted
A catalogue record for this book is available from the British Library

ISBN 0–7499–2123–4 (Hbk)
ISBN 0–7499–2188–9 (Pbk)

Text design by Paul Saunders
Edited by Carol Franklin

Set by Action Publishing Technology Ltd, Gloucester
Printed and bound in Great Britain by
Biddles Ltd, *www.biddles.co.uk*

Contents

Acknowledgements

There are a number of people who have been extremely supportive during the writing of this book. In particular, thanks go to my team at Speak First: Anne Wort who has managed to decipher my scrawl as I wrote and rewrote many chapters; and Gillian Gore, Caroline Blau and Simon Broomer who have kept everything going while I was absent.

Over the years our trainers have evolved and developed my original ideas and I would like especially to thank Clare Willis for her unflagging energy, Caroline Limpus for her contribution to the chapter on Voice, Rudi Szczerba for his comments on the Visual Aids chapters, Neil McNeil for the chapter on Dealing with the Media, and Isobel Jensen and Patrick Burke for their significant contribution over many years. Susie Kershaw's help was invaluable for the chapter regarding multicultural audiences.

Finally, I would like to acknowledge my editors, Katie Andrews and Gill Bailey, for their encouragement and guidance, without which this book would never have been written.

Introduction

In the last ten years a communications revolution has occurred in the workplace. Doing a good job is no longer enough. You must be able to express yourself, present ideas, win support, and above all, look confident. Of course, not everyone can do this. I am writing this book to help you make a positive impression and help you perform at your highest level when it matters most.

As jobs-for-life disappear and people move departments, companies, and even countries more often, they are frequently being asked to give presentations at their selection interviews. Even old hands are sent on presentation skills courses because they are now required to make presentations to colleagues and clients. Changes in many organisations mean that hierarchies have disappeared and people work in teams which re-form for every new project. Team members are expected to present on a regular basis. In just about every field, career advancement is difficult, if not impossible, without the ability to create and deliver effective presentations.

I firmly believe that everyone has the ability to be a good presenter. Unfortunately, in moments of pressure natural ability flies out of the window and you are left with sweaty palms, a pounding heart and a blank mind. I believe I know what changes you from an intelligent, articulate person under normal circumstances, into something else at the very moment when you want to appear at your best, and in this book I will show you how to stop this happening.

Over the past sixteen years I have met thousands of people in a state of nervous tension and yet, in a very short time, usually two days, they have developed calmness and confidence. They have learnt to believe in their innate ability to present well. They have attended one of our training courses.

I founded SpeakEasy Training (since 1999 known as Speak First) in 1985 because I felt that it was really unfortunate that so many people fail to gain recognition because they can't express themselves well. I have tried to distil my years of training experience into these pages so that you can benefit from them.

Why You Need This Book

This book is not about public speaking, it's about speaking in public. It will provide you with basic techniques you can apply in a variety of situations when you want to be listened to and when you need to be persuasive or convincing. For instance, you may hesitate about participating at a meeting and while you are thinking about the words someone else asks 'your question'; you may give instructions that are misunderstood; maybe your presentations to clients aren't winning as much new business as you would like; you may have recently been promoted to a position where you feel your colleagues are more articulate and fluent than you; or your sales may be down and you fear you aren't getting through to your sales force. Finally, you may already speak to large audiences and you want to appear more professional.

How to Use This Book

Probably, you have picked up this book because you have to give a presentation in the near future. The best way to learn the principles I have included is to apply them to an actual presentation. The first part is mostly about how to prepare *what* you want to say and how to illustrate it, and the second part is about *how* you say it, i.e. you, the presenter. The rest of the book covers more advanced techniques and a variety of different and difficult situations which you may face.

If you use the check list for preparation as you work on your own presentation, you will find you save time. You will also design a more logical, and therefore more easily understood, presentation if you follow the ideas in the chapters on How to Construct a Presentation and How to Hold an Audience.

Nobody is a 'Born Speaker'

We all admire speakers who can casually deliver a humorous, intelligent and well-reasoned talk apparently without trying. It's as effortless as a golf champion playing a winning shot, or an opera singer reaching the top note of an aria, or a comedian telling a successful joke.

It may appear effortless but, what we see is the culmination of months or even years of hard work and practice. Good speaking does not come without preparation, although to be effective, it should always appear so. It is a skill that can be learnt. You can learn to select essential points to persuade successfully, structure a talk so that your listeners will follow you easily and not be bored, hide nerves and uncertainty and show enthusiasm and sincerity. In addition, you can learn to develop an interesting speaking voice, make natural gestures and good eye contact, use visual aids and even cope with difficult questions. Nobody is born a good speaker. Remember what Emerson said: 'All the great speakers were bad speakers first.'

PART ONE

Preparation

1

What is Communication?

'The spoken word belongs half to the one who speaks it
and half to the one who hears it'
FRENCH PROVERB

Poor Listening

Communication is a two-way process. To be an effective
speaker you first need to understand how people listen.
Without this knowledge you could be broadcasting on the
wrong frequency and you wouldn't realise it – your message
may be clear and powerful, but is it being received?

Few people concentrate sufficiently when they are listening
and so they become distracted. Principally by their own
thoughts. This is sometimes called 'going down Route 350'.
The human mind processes words at a rate of approximately
500 a minute but we listen at about 150 words a minute – the
difference between the two is 350. When listeners 'switch off',
the chances are they are on Route 350. If you are sitting in a
long, tedious meeting you may be thinking about a difficult
problem that you have left on your desk and needs an immediate solution, while you are listening, or should I say half

listening, to what is being said by a speaker. You are going down Route 350.

Sometimes you're distracted because of something the speaker says. They may suggest a course of action you feel is unacceptable and you use your spare brain capacity to work out counter-arguments. Once again, you've set off down Route 350.

Most listeners are not like dry sponges ready to absorb everything the speaker gives them. They are continually assessing, digesting, rejecting or accepting what they hear. They are measuring it against their own bank of experience and prejudice and evaluating its worth. Is this going to work? Is that logical? What happens if I agree? Is this credible? Not only are they judging the content of what the speaker is saying, they are also judging the speaker. Why are they saying this? What's their experience? Do they seem to know what they're talking about?

So listeners sometimes fail to concentrate and can be distracted by their own thoughts, which may be unrelated to the speaker, or they may be distracted by what they are saying. They may also be distracted by their behaviour or appearance: 'Why does he keep taking off his glasses?... That's the twentieth "er" I've counted in five minutes!... Brown shoes with a grey suit ?... What awful taste!'

Reasons for Ineffective Listening

You may begin to wonder whether there is any point in your attempting to speak if no one is likely to listen to you, but bear with me because in the next section I'll describe the advantages of being a speaker.

For the moment, though, here are some other reasons why people may not be giving you their full attention:

• They anticipate what is going to be said and switch off.

• They are planning what to say when it's their turn.

- They may be tired or worried, i.e. they may have too much on their mind to concentrate.

- They can't hear or they find your voice dull and monotonous.

- The topic is too complex and difficult to follow or the topic is too simple and basic.

- You lack credibility, confidence and structure, and use too much jargon.

- The chairs are hard; it's either too hot or too cold; and the sound of the traffic is very distracting!

Is Writing a More Effective Communication Channel?

If you didn't speak in a business situation, how else could you communicate? The answer is probably by writing; so what's the difference between speaking and writing?

The major difference is that speakers can see their listeners. As a writer I can't see you, but I'd like to know whether you are still reading this section or whether you have skipped forward to another chapter. Because speakers can see their listeners, they can react to them. I can't react to you if you disagree with what you've read; I can't give you any additional examples or different arguments to convince you of my point.

Although readers have the freedom to absorb the author's message at their own pace and are able to reread complex passages, the author's words can't be changed to satisfy the readers' needs. By contrast, a speaker has the *flexibility* to alter and vary their message for different listeners; complex ideas can be re-explained using alternative words and phrases; the advantages and disadvantages of a course of action can be repeated giving a variety of examples; the listeners' own experiences can be used as support for the speaker's argument.

Your written memo might be misunderstood; your sales letter may go into the waste-paper basket; the recommendations in your report may be ignored, but if you present the same message in person, you are in a stronger position to ensure that it is understood, acknowledged and acted upon.

How to Make a Positive Impression as a Speaker

Although there are advantages in being present when you deliver your message, there are also pitfalls. Inexperienced speakers generally rely too heavily on words, probably because they feel more confident when writing than when speaking, so that they overlook other factors that give a successful speaker impact.

It has been estimated by Professor Albert Mehrabian, the communications researcher, that words account for only 7 per cent of the speaker's effect on an audience. A massive 55 per cent of the speaker's impact comes from the visual, i.e. how they look, facial expression, gestures, body language and posture, etc.; while 38 per cent of the impact comes from voice – Does the speaker sound trustworthy? Is the speaker's voice varied and interesting to listen to? This breakdown of the effect that a speaker has on a listener may sound unlikely to you. So, imagine a situation where you have returned a faulty item to a store. The shop assistant says, 'I'm sorry. I'll see what we can do.' If this is said in a disinterested voice as the assistant leans on the counter about to resume a conversation with another assistant you won't feel confident that very much will happen. On the other hand, the same words expressed with concern by an assistant who is standing up straight and looking directly at you will create an entirely different impression.

Here is another example. Think back to your favourite teacher or tutor at school or university. The first person who comes to mind is probably someone who was enthusiastic and animated; not a person who only relied on words, but also someone with vocal and visual impact.

If you feel you usually don't notice very much about a speaker's voice, try recalling any phone calls you've made to people who are unknown to you. I am sure you made judgements and assessments based on their voices – she sounded friendly or angry or ineffectual; he was aggressive or honest or happy. Most of the time you will find you are making these evaluations of people unconsciously.

In the same way listeners make evaluations of speakers. They might say, 'He seemed ill at ease' or 'She looked very confident'. Often these opinions are formed before the speaker has said one word and are based entirely on the visual impact. Some speakers look inspiring and enthusiastic, while others appear dull and insipid. Based on this visual impression listeners will have made up their minds as to whether it's worthwhile paying attention to them.

So, remember that *how* you speak is often as important as what you say. A sound and well-reasoned talk can be ruined by bad presentation, while a poorly constructed or unoriginal talk seems entertaining and convincing if presented with vitality.

Different Techniques: Writing Versus Speaking

Throughout this book, I'm going to draw the distinction between speaking and writing because it's often wrongly assumed that the skills of writing can be applied to speaking. You should also be aware of the difference between listening and reading so that you can adjust your approach and successfully reach your audience.

Writer	Speaker
• Writer can't see reader.	• Speaker can see listener.

- Writer can't react.

- Speaker can slow down/ speed up/repeat and involve listeners.

- Writer relies on words alone.

- Speaker can use body language and voice for emphasis, enthusiasm and emotion.

- Writer can carefully choose words, but cannot change them.

- Speaker can be more flexible and relevant by modifying and altering words and phrases to suit the listeners.

- Writer explains topic only once and reader can reread.

- Speaker must have a simple, easy-to-follow structure, frequent summaries and relevant examples because listeners can't relisten.

A Final Thought

After a 10-minute talk listeners will have understood and re-tained approximately half of what was said and a couple of days later they'll only remember about a quarter.

SUMMARY

- Learn how to become a more effective listener.

- Remember a speaker has the flexibility to alter their message for different audiences.

- Create a positive impression – keep in mind that how you speak is as important as what you say.

2

Preparing and Planning a Presentation

'I am the most spontaneous speaker in the world because every word, every gesture, and every retort has been carefully rehearsed'

GEORGE BERNARD SHAW

How to Start

The deadline approaches and you finally sit down in front of your PC, determined to start preparing your talk, unable to find any more excuses for putting it off. You search for inspiration and desperately seek an opening line. Alternatively, you may start with your visual aids. If you're preparing for a large meeting, you may skim through a book of jokes because humour is supposed to 'warm up' the audience, but nothing seems appropriate. You may try three or four different opening paragraphs that all end up in the waste-paper bin. I'm not surprised, because you are starting in the wrong place.

> *Proper preparation and practice prevent poor performance*

Researching Your Audience

Before you start your journey you need to consider your fellow travellers, because paths that may be suitable for one group may be inappropriate for another, and you will lose them before you reach your destination.

You may be reading this book because you need to speak at departmental meetings of eight people, or you may anticipate addressing a conference of 80 or 800 participants. So, through the rest of the book, I'm going to use the word 'audience' to describe *anyone* who is listening to you speak. You may feel that a bunch of your workmates doesn't constitute an audience, but if you are speaking to them at a business meeting, that is exactly what they are.

Whether your audience is large or small, if you're going to be an effective speaker, you must find out as much as possible about them. Have you ever had the experience of listening to a talk where nothing the speaker said was relevant to you? You found the material unoriginal and self-evident and from the shuffling and inattentive audience, you judged that they felt the same as you. In fact, there was probably nothing wrong with the talk at all; it was simply given to the wrong audience.

You can toss a cricket ball at a dartboard and hit the bull's-eye, but it won't stick. In the same way, you may be speaking well, but is it sticking? Are you using the right words for your listeners? Are you structuring what you have to say so that they will understand easily? Are your illustrations relevant? Deciding whether to throw a cricket ball, a dart, a javelin or even a hammer is one of the skills of speaking. Choosing what you're going to throw depends on what you want to hit.

A group of bank managers asked me to advise them on the presentations they were giving to school leavers. Naturally they hoped to encourage these young men and women to open bank accounts, but somehow they weren't having the success they hoped for. It was hardly surprising. These middle-aged men didn't realise the need to understand their audience. It was no good talking about security, savings and pensions to a group of people who were longing to spend, spend, spend. Once the bank managers made their talk *relevant* to sixteen-year-olds, their presentations were successful.

Finding out about your audience will enable you to make your talk relevant to them and thereby overcome many of the difficulties that listeners face when trying to follow the spoken word: you should plan your journey according to your fellow travellers.

What you need to know about your audience

You know why you are speaking, but do *they*? So ask yourself the following questions:

- Why are they there?

- What do they expect?

- What do they want or need?

- What's their level of knowledge?

- What is their attitude likely to be to you and your views?

- Have they any past experiences that will influence them towards or against you?

And if you are speaking to larger, external audiences, you will need to find out additional information, as set out below.

Why are they there?

If you're speaking at a meeting in your own workplace it is possible your audience has no choice about attending: they are there because it's the Friday afternoon meeting; or because there is a threat that a major client is going to move their account; or it's the distribution department's monthly meeting.

Sometimes you have invited your audience to listen to you, for example you are making a sales presentation to a prospective customer. Alternatively, a client may have asked you to give a progress report on their project. At a public conference, your audience may have paid to attend.

Ask yourself whether your audience have chosen to listen to you and are there of their own free will, or whether they were sent – this can make a significant difference in their attitude towards you. Occasionally I find myself facing a group of antagonistic managers who feel resentful that they have been sent on yet another useless course when they have a desk full of problems to be solved. They are not receptive to my training and begrudge the time wasted on the course. When I am aware of this attitude I try to overcome it.

What do they expect?

You must satisfy your audiences expectations – if they are expecting a report on your experience with flexitime for office staff, telling them about the problems you have finding a suitable garage to service the company vans will not be relevant. A group of business people expecting a light-hearted after-lunch speech will not welcome a plea for more money to be spent on training for young people in industry. In both cases the audience might well be interested in the alternative talk, but if it is not what they were expecting, they will not be receptive listeners.

When a client engages me to teach effective speaking, I know I can spend an amusing morning telling them of some of the disasters I have faced in my speaking career. It would be entertaining but inappropriate if they were expecting to be taught; they might learn from my mistakes, but I would not be teaching them.

Beware of confusing your objective with your audience's expectations. They are not the same. A travel agent client gave a presentation in which he identified his objective as: 'To convince the audience that Spain has more interesting holiday resorts than Greece.' He started his talk by saying 'I'm going to convince you that . . .' No audience wants to be *told* that. They want to make up their own minds. In the above example the audience wanted to be informed about the relative merits of Greek and Spanish holiday resorts. The speaker may be certain of convincing them, but the audience resents being told so, and will erect a mental barrier against the speaker's arguments. A better start might have been: 'I'd like to give you information about Spain and Greece to help you decide which is most attractive for you.'

What do they want or need?

To achieve your objective, or reach your destination with all your fellow travellers, you must make the journey relevant to them. Your message must satisfy their needs. This doesn't mean that you change the content of your message, but simply that you put yourself in your audience's shoes and present it from their point of view.

I heard a manager arguing that he should have a mobile phone because all the other managers on his grade had one. His request was refused. He didn't think about the listener's needs. He should have pointed out to his boss that currently he was wasting considerable time looking for functioning public telephones in order to keep in touch with his office, and that on occasions he had arrived at cancelled meetings because his secretary couldn't reach him. He could have said, 'My wasted time is costing you a lot of money – with a mobile phone I would be more efficient.'

In general you can be fairly sure that one or more of the management needs listed below should be satisfied by your argument:

• saving money;

• increasing productivity and efficiency;

- saving time;

- improving quality.

If you are talking to your workforce, you may find that other needs are paramount:

- earning more money;

- recognition of work effort;

- security of employment;

- job satisfaction;

- career advancement.

This is by no means a complete list; you'll be able to identify the needs of your own audience when you start to think about them in this way.

I had to advise a local government client who was unable to convince applicants for grants of the importance of accurate form-filling. Each form submitted had miscalculations, omissions and incorrect information which were causing more work for everyone concerned. Although the applicants had been told several times that the forms were important, they continued to fill them in with careless mistakes. I suggested the client look at it from the applicants' point of view. What did they want? What were their needs? The answer was that the applicants wanted their grants as quickly as possible. The next question was how to satisfy this need? The answer, of course, was by accurate form-filling; and the client went on to explain how this could be achieved. When the applicants were shown how they could benefit from following the instructions, they were prepared to listen.

If you are facing an unwilling audience, you'll need to tell them at the beginning of your talk how they will benefit from listening to you. In order to do this, you must, of course, know their needs. With reluctant managers on my courses, I tell them that I can show them how to save time preparing their talks; how they need never fear boring an audience; how I can teach them to overcome nervousness; and how they can look and sound more professional. At the end of this little speech, I hope I have gained their attention and overcome their reluctance to be there.

What's their level of knowledge?

Here are some more questions you must ask as part of your audience research:

- How much do they already know about the topic?

- How much do they think they know?

- How much do they want to know?

- How much do they need to know so that you achieve the result you want?

The last question is the most important, but you can only answer it when you have some idea of the knowledge they have already. If you were explaining how new legislation could affect your company, you would choose a different starting point if you were addressing the personnel director than if you were talking to the warehouse manager. You may have been part of an audience or group at which the speaker assumed a common background knowledge which *you* didn't have and consequently you found it difficult to follow the arguments. Alternatively, if you are familiar with a subject, it can be equally irritating to listen to fulsome explanations. In both situations, if the speaker has not done sufficient audience research, it will be impossible to make the message relevant and listeners will go off wandering down Route 350. The uninformed group will try to fathom out the speaker's meaning; the more knowledgeable one will be bored by the content.

In a situation where you are aware that there will be a varied level of knowledge, you can give enough background information to enable everyone to understand your talk. For example, 'You'll probably remember that the dip in sales revenue last October was due to the cancellation of the large Australian order. I think we need to bear this in mind when looking at these figures.'

Avoid using phrases like 'For the benefit of those who don't know . . .' or 'For the less experienced among you . . .' No one wants to be identified (even to him- or herself) as one of the ignorant.

What is their attitude likely to be to you and your views?

In favour? Against? Indifferent? Open-minded?

If, before you speak, you are aware of any negative attitudes, you can attempt to overcome objections within your talk: 'You may be wondering how we can achieve this without taking on more staff . . .', 'If this sounds like an expensive proposal, may I suggest you look at it this way . . .', 'Many people say I look too young to have enough experience to cope with the problems of this department . . .'

Have they any past experiences that will influence them towards or against you?

Bad experiences colour people's judgements and often create an invisible barrier that prevents your message from being received and understood. You must acknowledge and remove this obstacle if you are to reach your destination with your listeners: 'I know that a similar experiment using temporary staff failed last year, but let me show you how my scheme is different', 'Some of you may have given up using an outside contractor because of the communication problems that it posed. We can prevent this happening by . . .'

Check list for speaking to external audiences

On occasion you may be asked to speak outside your own workplace as a panellist, a guest speaker or a workshop leader chairing a discussion, or as an after-lunch or dinner speaker. The more you can discover about the audience and the location, the more confident and effective you will be as a speaker. This check list will help you.

Who?

Find out about your audience; ask your contact all the specific questions listed below:

- How many will be present?

- What is their position/occupation/title?

- What is their background/education/culture/race?

- What is their sex, male/female/male and female?

- What is their age?

Where?

Make sure your know the exact address and telephone number, available parking, nearest railway station/airport. What type of room/hall/office/conference centre will you be in?

When?

What is the day of the week, the date and the exact time?

What?

What is the topic and any specific angle, as well as the reason for inviting you?

How?

Will there be a stage/lectern? Is there a microphone and, if so, what type? What equipment is available? How will the audience be sitting? In rows/a semi-circle/with tables?

Duration?
How long should you speak and does this include question time? When will the questions be taken? Will there be a panel discussion?

Other speakers?
Names and telephone numbers of any other speakers would be useful.

See also Chapter 15 Writing and Reading Scripts for Conferences for more advice on this topic.

Setting an Objective

Now you have researched your fellow travellers, you can concentrate on your destination. You need to know where you are heading and where you want to get to – in other words, what is the objective of your presentation? Later, you choose your path but if you don't know where you are going, it is difficult to decide how to get there.

Before you even consider what you want to say, you must ask yourself, 'Why am I speaking?' What do you want to achieve? How do you want your listeners to feel when you have finished? What is the reaction you most want from your audience? Allow yourself to daydream on the ideal outcome of your talk. Don't worry about whether it's likely, or even possible, at this stage; simply identify what you want to accomplish.

Sometimes clients find it difficult to pinpoint exactly what they want to achieve. They tell me, 'I'm speaking because it's the Annual Sales Conference', 'I'm speaking because I've been told to', 'I'm speaking because I am the Chairman', 'I'm speaking because it's my turn', and so on. If you are unsure how to identify your objectives, here are some pointers.

Start with general objectives

General objectives fall into the following categories:

- to inform/teach/train;
- to stimulate/motivate/inspire;
- to persuade/convince/sell;
- to explore/debate/negotiate;
- to amuse/entertain.

Writing down your objective in clear, precise terms is often difficult, but if you refer to the general objectives, they should help you. Remember that you will sometimes need to combine several objectives. When I speak to the personnel team of a large company about my training courses, my objective is *to sell* training to them. However, I also *inform* them of the content of the courses, *inspire* them with stories of previous successes, *motivate* them by showing them how economical our training is in comparison with other companies, *persuade* them with logical arguments and even *shame* them by pointing out how poorly their company's staff perform compared with those in other organisations. Remember that one general objective should predominate; don't confuse yourself with a mixture of too many general objectives, but always aim to include some entertainment.

Do write out your objective. Remember it must be *specific*, but also *achievable*. If your objective is to convince your boss you should have a company car (which may be an achievable objective), don't insist that it should be a Rolls-Royce (probably an unachievable objective).

I advised a hospital manager on a speech she was giving to a convention of doctors. She was concerned that she had nothing new to say and that she would bore her audience. She was unable to find the means to straighten out a jumble of thoughts until I asked her what changes in their behaviour she would like to inspire. Suddenly she saw how she could prepare a very passionate speech on doctors' attitudes towards nursing staff. Once she had an objective her thoughts became directed and fell into a logical sequence. When she had decided her destination, she was able to choose her route to it.

Another client, a managing director of a family-owned business, annually 'addressed the troops' (his words). Each year he spoke for 20 minutes and although for many of his staff this was the only occasion when they saw him, most of them considered it to be a boring waste of time. I asked him how he would like his staff to feel after he had spoken. For some time he talked vaguely of motivation and productivity and feeling happy at work and finally he said he wanted them to understand how much he genuinely needed them. We then started to look at how he could achieve this. He had a destination, so he could start examining the various paths that might lead there.

You may be saying to yourself, that's all very well for anyone who needs to speak in public, but you only need to speak at internal meetings. I suggest that, before your next meeting, you set aside a few minutes to think about objectives and answer the question, what do you want to accomplish by speaking? Is it to convince colleagues that your ideas are better than theirs? Do you want to stimulate a sales force? Maybe you want to impress your boss. Be honest and find your real objective. It should be:

- written down;

- specific;

- achievable.

Where's the action?

As you set out your objective, be sure to identify exactly what you want to achieve and how you will measure whether or not you have been successful. Sometimes an *action* will follow. In selling, you know you have achieved your objective when the customer agrees to buy. You also can have a fall-back position or a *secondary objective*; you may not make a sale, but your customer gives you the names of several companies which might be interested in your product. Your boss may not agree to a company car immediately, but does agree to you having one in six months.

You may find that identifying the reaction you want from your listeners helps you to set an objective. I talked to a manager who had been asked to speak at a convention which was to be attended by politicians, members of the press and senior representatives of his industry. As he was uncertain as to what he should say, I asked what he would like them to do as a result of what he had said. He found lots of actions, so he started from the action and worked backwards. To identify the action, you must ask yourself how you want people *to behave* or what you want people *to do* after they have heard you speak. An office supervisor may identify the action he requires as 'a decrease in the number of telephone calls put through to the wrong extension'. His objectives might eventually look like this:

- to instruct the switchboard operators on the new telephone equipment;

- to motivate them to take a pride in their job so that fewer phone calls are put through to the wrong extension.

When you have completed this first stage of your preparation, you should have a clear and concisely written objective which answers the question:

> *Why am I speaking and what do I want the outcome to be?*

You might be tempted to skip this step as it can be time-consuming to write down a succinctly worded objective that is achievable and honest. But the time and effort you spend on objective setting now will be saved later on in your preparation as it will be easier to select material and identify key points.

Brain-storm Your Ideas

So far in your preparation you've discovered as much as you can about your fellow travellers and you have chosen your destination. Your third step is to study the map. What routes will be most effective in helping you reach your destination? What material should you include in your talk to help you achieve your objective?

You may need to speak in a variety of different situations, but the method I'm going to describe for researching your material can probably be applied equally well to all of them. From now on I will refer to your 'talk', although you may actually be making a presentation, giving instructions, leading a training group, presenting a report or making a speech.

When you have been asked to give a talk, the usual reaction is 'Why me? I don't have anything to say.' When the initial panic has died down, you'll probably realise that you have a great deal to say and your real problem is deciding what to leave out.

Freeing the mind

I expect most of your original ideas come to you at inconvenient moments like driving on the motorway in the fast lane, under the shower or in the middle of the night. I'm going to show you a method of capturing interesting ideas when it's most convenient for you.

Unfortunately, much of our education has trained us to think in a logical and linear manner. As you sit in front of your PC or with a blank piece of paper in front of you to prepare your talk, you may even start with a (i) in the margin, but most ideas don't arrive in a numbered sequence; it's difficult if not impossible to be creative and structured at the same time. So, instead of forcing your creativity into a linear structure, draw a circle in the centre of your paper and write in it the subject of your talk and, as you let your mind free-wheel around it, jot down any ideas that come to you. Place your ideas on lines radiating from the central topic. You'll find that each idea triggers off others so that you can continuously build on them. The advantage of this mind map (see over) is that you have plenty of space to add new thoughts and you can also expand on those you have already jotted down. You'll have to avoid the temptation to reject material before you have written it down. This is *not* an evaluation exercise. It is simply a method of brain-storming with yourself so you can put on paper everything that you know about your subject. You mustn't assess whether the material is relevant or logical – that can come later. I find that if I build the mind map over several days, new thoughts and angles occur to me at odd moments during that period.

Sometimes when I suggest a mind map to clients, they dislike the concept, finding it messy or confused. At this stage that doesn't matter. It's more important to follow through thoughts, views, opinions and information that may lead to examples and illustrations, that in turn will help your listeners to understand your talk.

Too often people curb their creativity when they judge material as unsuitable or when they decide that it doesn't fit a predetermined structure. With a mind map, there are no restrictions, and every idea and thought has equal merit.

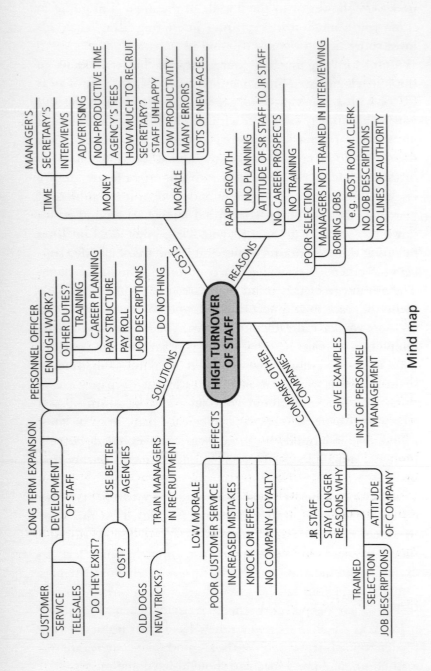

Mind map

Selection

If you didn't like the untidiness of the mind map, you'll appreciate the next stage in your preparation. Now you must look at the map and decide which paths or ideas are most suitable for your fellow travellers so that you can all reach your destination together.

First, look at your objective and at your audience profile. Ask yourself what material you need to achieve your objective, knowing what you do about the audience.

You must assess each idea against your objective, always bearing in mind how your audience is likely to react. An idea that is totally convincing for a group of middle-aged business men may not be appropriate for young male and female graduate trainees.

I once heard a sales trainer advising a predominantly female audience that rugby and cricket clubs were useful places in which to extend their range of contacts. Good advice maybe, but not necessarily for that audience. So your first criterion must be to select material that is relevant to your audience, and that will make it easier for you to achieve your objective.

Secondly, refer back to your audience's needs. How can you satisfy them? Can you present your report in such a way as to show that your recommendations will save the company money? Can you persuade your staff to accept the new schedules by offering them greater job satisfaction? Are you addressing a large audience consisting of people who want to achieve recognition in their own field? Any audience will want to know what's in it for them, so select material that will satisfy their needs and their expectations.

Be very selective

If you overload your talk with too many good points, your audience will forget them all. Remember that after a couple of days they will only have retained approximately a quarter of what you have said. You will be more effective if you choose one or two points, develop them, present supporting evidence, choose relevant illustrations, and recap and summarise frequently.

SUMMARY

- Who is going to listen? Find out about the audience.

- Brain-storm a mind map. Don't be judgemental; be creative.

- Select ideas. Choose a few key points to achieve your objective.

- In other words, get to know your fellow travellers, choose your destination, study the map and finally choose the paths that will take you there together.

3

How to Construct a Presentation

'Good order is the foundation of all things'
EDMUND BURKE (*Reflections on the Revolution in France*, 1790)

This chapter will look at how you can choose a logical structure to help your listeners follow your talk, develop key ideas and add supporting material, as well as illustrations and examples. By the end of this chapter you should be able to construct a persuasive and entertaining talk or presentation.

Organise Your Main Points

Listeners find it difficult to concentrate on the spoken word, so you must give them a framework. This is the equivalent of a contents page in a book or chapter headings and sub-headings for paragraphs. If you announce your structure early on in your talk, your listeners will be able to refer back to it if they wander down Route 350 from time to time. By summarising after each of your points, you can lead them back on to the main track with you. Remember that they can't reread your previous paragraph so you need to help them when their concentration fails.

Deciding on a structure

Your structure must be logical, simple to follow and relevant to your audience. Here are some types of structure you can use.

Problem/solution

This is a common structure often used in business presentations in which an examination of the problem is followed by a proposed solution. If you are suffering a high turnover of staff, you could describe the problem and show how to resolve it by proposing a more selective recruiting programme. If your company has a low profile in the trade press, you could outline the current situation and suggest a public relations campaign to improve its image. A variation on this structure can be used when you are in a competitive situation: describe the problem, examine a number of possible solutions, pointing out the weaknesses of each, and finally present your own solution emphasising all the advantages.

Chronological structure

In this method the key points are given in a natural time-sequence order. For instance, you could state the origins of the problem and how it developed over the course of a number of years. This is useful if you want to set it in its historical context. It is also helpful when you are instructing or training, as you can demonstrate the sequence of steps or stages in a particular process. Audiences find it easy to follow a logical time pattern. However, this doesn't allow you to indicate the importance of one idea in relation to another. Your second and fourth points may be more important than the points preceding them, but this won't be apparent from the order in which you present them. You can overcome this disadvantage in your final conclusion by emphasising the areas you feel are most significant.

Topical structure

Also known as the qualitative structure, when you use the topical structure you list your points in their order of significance with the most important at the beginning. This is useful when you think your audience may not concentrate through your entire talk and are likely to pay more attention in the first few minutes. Generally, the listener's attention is keenest at the beginning of a talk and therefore it's prudent to take advantage of this. Remember that, in selecting your most telling or vital idea, you must refer back to your objective.

Spatial structure

In this structure you can either begin with the particular and move to the general or, alternatively, examine the big picture first and then show how it applies to the audience. For example, you may want to analyse the sales pattern for the past six months and then put it into the context of the previous three years. You could present new taxation legislation in broad terms and then explain how it would apply in two particular situations.

Theory/practice

In this structure you outline the theory and then show how it works in practice. It's often beneficial to link the theory to what the audience already knows about the subject and then progress on to the less familiar. I saw a trainer instructing a young group of new employees in basic telephone manners. He asked them to recall situations when they had been treated well on the telephone and also occasions when they had had to wait unnecessarily. He checked what impression they had of the companies with which they had been dealing. From their personal experience he was able to demonstrate the importance of dealing efficiently with members of the public on the telephone. He went on to show them the techniques they should use in future on the telephone, in order to create a positive company image.

Finding the correct order

It is helpful to choose a suitable structure at this stage in your preparation, because it enables you to place your ideas in the correct order. If you are undecided on your structure, try writing out your main points on several small cards so that you can physically move them about and experiment with a variety of different sequences.

Expand and Explain Principal Ideas

The next preparation step will depend on the type of talk you are giving. If you are merely speaking for a few minutes at an internal meeting, you may find that you only need to note down a few selected points from your mind map, choose the sequence that will be most logical for your audience, and your preparation will be complete.

Alternatively, if you are addressing a conference of several hundred people, or bidding for a vital contract, you will want to plan in more detail how you can develop and support your main points and present them in the most positive way.

Think around your key ideas. If your colleagues have some experience of the topic, talk to them, as an exchange of views can often stimulate a new train of thought; do write down any of the examples or illustrations that will help you to emphasise a particular point.

Occasionally, when I am preparing a talk, I use a tape recorder at this stage. Imagine a member of your audience is seated in front of you and you have the opportunity of speaking to that person on a one-to-one basis. Switch on your tape recorder and talk around your key points. At first you will feel inhibited, but persevere as you may find that talking aloud opens up previously untapped areas of material and releases ideas you had stored at the back of your mind. Remember that the purpose of this exercise is to expand the key ideas you have already selected; you should be researching ways of presenting these main points so that your audience is totally involved and persuaded by you. Try to avoid adding new main points at this juncture. A rough guide is one point per 5 minutes with a maximum of five points in 30 minutes. You should avoid speaking for more than 20 minutes, but if this isn't possible, consider using two or three speakers to add variety.

Each of your key ideas is a mini speech and needs to be introduced, developed and concluded; they should be linked together and should have two or three minor points to support them. If you want to write out your talk, some of the suggestions in Chapter 15 Writing and Reading Scripts for Conferences may help you. Alternatively, you can write down your main points on white cards (see 'How to write confidence cards' in Chapter 7 Delivering Your Talk).

Add Colour and Sweeteners

Once you have written or outlined the body of your talk, try to identify where the dull patches occur; you are unlikely to maintain a high level of concentration from your listeners throughout your talk and therefore you need to add colour and sweeteners to stimulate their interest. The graph overleaf demonstrates this.

Aim for a variety of facts, personal illustrations, examples and explanations. It's this mixture that holds an audience's attention. Some of your material may be heavy and difficult to digest, so intersperse it with some real-life examples to make it more acceptable to your audience. Try to break up chunks of essential but dry information with illustrations that are

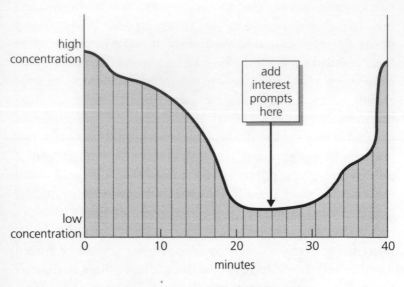

concentration

add
interest
prompts
here

low
concentration

0   10   20   30   40

minutes

Concentration curve of audiences

relevant to your listeners. Ask yourself whether some of your points could be better explained with the use of a visual aid. Remember that a visual aid should be a visual expression of an idea that is difficult to describe with words alone. It should not be a repetition of the words you have spoken. Ask yourself whether your audience would find it easier to follow your talk if they had a handout or a chart or a table of figures to refer to. See also Chapter 5 How to Design Visual Aids and Chapter 6 How to Look Professional When Using Visual Aids.

Is there a natural break between two points where it would be worth while asking the audience some questions? Are there any other techniques involving the audience that you could use to break up the presentation? Even changing your physical position helps the audience to maintain their attention. Too much movement is distracting, but an occasional change of your position from one side of the room or platform to the other enables the audience to refocus.

You only need to consider these suggestions for varying the mixture within your talk if you are speaking for over 5 minutes. Under this time the content should be sufficient to keep your listeners alert.

Example: Alan Glanville's Presentation

The illustration of the mind map on page 24 shows how one manager brain-stormed the problem of a constant turnover of staff that his company faced. On his mind map Alan Glanville jotted down all aspects of the problem, together with his ideas for solving it. He wanted to convince his board of directors that the company needed to employ a trained personnel officer, but he knew that they considered this an unnecessary expense for a company of their size.

Alan decided that a problem/solution structure most suited his 10-minute presentation but he also wanted to make use of some of the other structures to develop his key points. He felt that, as the overriding objection to employing a personnel officer was financial, he needed to show how much the continual recruitment of staff had cost the company in the past.

- Alan's objective: To convince the board of directors that the company could save time and money and create a happier and more productive workforce by appointing a personnel officer.

- How did he achieve this objective? By demonstrating the real cost of recruiting staff under the present system.

- What action did he want which would indicate that he had achieved his objective? Agreement for him to place an advertisement for a personnel officer.

Below is the outline for his talk showing how he developed each of his key points:

1 The problem

(a) How it developed (chronological structure, past–present)

Small, family-run company with loyal staff; sudden, rapid growth; inadequate job descriptions; poorly recruited new staff; insufficient training; dissatisfaction and low morale among employees.

(b) Cost in time and money of recruiting (spatial structure)

Cost of advertisements; secretary's time handling responses to advertisements; manager's time interviewing candidates; non-productive time for training.

Use a flip chart to show true costs of recruiting one secretary. In one year 30 junior staff replaced, e.g. post-room clerk changed five times. Show total cost over a twelve-month period of recruiting 30 people.

(c) Why don't staff stay longer? (topical structure)

Poor recruitment because managers not trained as interviewers; unclear lines of authority, e.g. warehouse packing clerk should help postroom on busy days, but who decides? Poor job descriptions, e.g. relief work on switchboard done as a favour and causes resentment; no formal wages structure, e.g. pay increases apparently given at the whim of manager, resulting in complaints of favouritism; staff with the company for three years accused of not welcoming newcomers; senior staff don't know names of junior staff.

2 The solution

(d) Personnel Officer (chronological structure, present–future)

Show main advantages to solving the current problem; overcome any objections regarding costs, i.e. refer to the high cost of recruiting new staff. Other advantages: some departments will be more productive as some aspects of their present work will be handled by personnel officer, e.g. accounts department and the pay roll, secretaries will not be involved in recruiting; central pay structure – fewer complaints; proper job descriptions – less friction; recruiting with career development in mind, e.g. customer service department currently handles telephoned complaints, with sales training they could develop telephone selling skills; long-term planning and expansion easier without present difficulties.

You can see from the above example how Alan selected some of the key ideas and developed them to achieve his objective.

He chose to use the flip chart to demonstrate the actual cost of recruiting one secretary, as spoken numbers are difficult to comprehend and retain. If a flip chart hadn't been available, he could have prepared a handout showing a breakdown of his calculations to help his audience follow his arguments.

In order that his presentation should not become too theoretical, he gave several examples and illustrations to make it come alive for his listeners, e.g. changing the postroom clerk five times.

Although all the ideas on his mind map were valid and interesting, you will see that because he wanted to speak only for 10 minutes he had to reject some of them, but he made sure that the file that he took to the meeting contained the additional information in case he was asked questions about it.

Later on in this chapter you will see how Alan chose to begin and conclude his presentation.

How to Start

You may have forgotten that this was the title of the first section in Chapter 2 Preparing and Planning a Presentation. As you can see, you need to spend sufficient time and effort on the body of your talk before you reach the stage where you can choose your opening sentences.

Making Your First Impression

In some ways your opening words are the most important. Although people only half-listen to the content, it's at this stage that they are assessing how much of their mental energy you deserve. You will already have made a first impression before you actually say a single word and as they hear your voice (maybe for the first time) you will be failing or passing the next test. How interesting are you? Are you worth listening to? Do you have *enthusiasm, sincerity* and *vitality*?

Your first few words must create a stillness as the audience prick up their ears and wait for your next sentence. You must grab their attention and suspend their mental questioning. Your opening words must be imaginative, stimulating and above all attention gaining. Don't confuse your opening words with the introduction to your subject. That comes later. If you feel that this sounds too theatrical for your business presentation, don't dismiss the concept completely; look at the examples below and consider whether you could use one or several of them to make your next talk more entertaining.

Your opening words to your audience must be enticing, seductive and should make them want to listen to you. You need to capture their attention, stop their minds wandering and show them you're worth listening to. It's a tall order, but essential if you expect to achieve your objectives.

It's as simple as A, B, C and D:

Attention – capture their attention

Benefits – show them what they will gain from listening

Credentials – give them your credentials for speaking

Direction and destination – tell them your structure

This may seem a lot to fit into one paragraph, but it can be covered in less than a minute. I have described these four ingredients in more detail below, because from my own experience I know that your opening few sentences can be crucial to the success of your talk.

Attention-getting techniques

Ask a question

- 'Do you know how many phone calls the accounts department receives every day?'

- 'Can you remember what you were doing on Tuesday 11 August last year?'

- 'Have you any idea how many hours you spend in your car each week?'

As you read through those questions, you may have quickly thought of your own answers and that is what the audience does, or else they listen for an answer from the speaker. Questions engage the minds of the audience and make them concentrate. *Don't* make your opening question too involved otherwise they will be working out the answer and won't be listening to your next sentence; *do* make the question relevant to the audience.

Quotation

- 'The brain is a wonderful organ – it begins working the moment you are born and goes on working perfectly until the moment that you have to stand up and speak in public.'

- 'There are two kinds of men who never amount to much; those who cannot do what they are told and those who can do nothing else.'

- 'Doing business without advertising is like winking in the dark – you know what you are doing but no one else does.'

Bookshops and libraries are full of books of quotations and you'll find you can spend hours looking for an appropriate opening for your talk. Many of the modern dictionaries of quotations are compiled by subject and this reduces your research time. Some quotes benefit from your giving their source and you can preface your remark something along the lines of 'I like the advice that Mark Twain gave on public speaking "The right word may be effective, but no word can ever be as effective as a mighty, timed pause."' Other speakers are often a source of pithy and amusing quotations, so keep a file of interesting ones that you can refer to when you get stuck.

Anecdotes

A short story that launches you quickly into the subject matter of your talk is useful, provided it is relevant to the audience and to your topic. Here is an extract from a story I heard at a meeting of personnel managers in which the speaker introduced his talk by describing the impossibly high expectations of some of the applicants for a recently advertised job:

> 'One young man said that he liked the sound of the job but that at his last employment he was paid more and the conditions were better. I asked him what they were and he told me that he was given free life insurance, was enrolled in a private health scheme and that every year there was a 10 per cent bonus at Christmas, together with six weeks' paid holiday a year, free travel and every Friday they finished at 3 p.m. I said to him, "It sounds perfect, why on earth did you leave?" He looked at me sheepishly and said "They went bust."'

On another occasion I heard a speaker open his talk on business acumen with this true story:

> 'Once upon a time there were two soft drinks companies. One got into deep financial trouble and the other was offered the opportunity to buy them out. The successful company figured the unsuccessful one couldn't last long and turned down the takeover opportunity. The successful company was Coca-Cola and the other one was Pepsi. Somewhere someone must be kicking himself.'

If you are using second-hand material, try to personalise it so that it appears to be your own experience. But it is generally better to use your own stories, provided you cut out any irrelevant detail. In Chapter 12 Using Humour Successfully, you'll see that the most successful anecdotes are those you tell against yourself.

Shock openings

These can be fun, but you must be confident and deliver your words carefully so that their full impact is felt by the audience. For instance try, 'You are wasting your time sitting here listening to me [pause] unless you're prepared to act on my suggestions.' Here is another: 'There is an epidemic in Britain that can't be cured by doctors but it's responsible for more lost worker-hours in British industry than any other. Doctors can't cure it, but we managers can. I'm talking about backache.'

Historical background

This is a suitable beginning to set the context for a speech with a chronological structure: 'Twenty years ago this hall was a field and the idea for an industrial estate was being ferociously debated in the Town Hall.'

Current affairs

Sometimes a news item provides the right peg on which to hang your talk. Be careful not to use an item that has only just appeared in the news bulletins, as your listeners may not have heard it. You can find this opening useful if you are visiting a town and you refer to a local story; your audience will feel that you are taking an interest in their area and not just passing through. However, remember to comment in a favourable way.

The benefits – what's in it for them?

Once you have gained your listeners' attention, you must tell them why they should continue to listen to you. In other words show them what's in it for them. This only needs a few words, but it reinforces the impression that you are worth their mental energy. Refer back to your audience research to find out what their needs and wants are, because when you describe the benefit it must be specific to them.

Here is an example of how a general manager began his talk when he was addressing a sales conference: 'We are going to double your commission and halve your targets this year. You may think that I have got that round the wrong way. I'm going to describe a new product that is so good that you'll only need to put in half the effort for twice the rewards.'

At a client presentation the manager of a mailing house company described to her client how she had reduced a competitor's mailing costs by half and promised that she could do the same for them.

In both these instances the audience may only half believe what they hear but nevertheless they are prepared to pay attention to the speaker. I had the experience of attending a conference for trainers where one of the speakers told us that she could show us how to save an hour a day if we followed her method of time management. I certainly wanted an extra hour in my day and so I could see the benefit in listening to what she had to say.

Credentials – establish your credibility

In your next sentence you should tell your audience why you are qualified to speak on that subject, in other words, what is your experience? A few words usually suffice to demonstrate that you are the right person. For instance, a systems analyst was addressing a school board. 'During the last four years I have personally supervised the computerisation of records in eight large schools in the region so I know the kind of problems that you are facing here.' At an insurance investigators' conference a speaker explained his experience to the audience like this: 'While I was in the States I researched the methods being used there to detect fraud in insurance claims so that I am now in a position to compare their methods with ours.'

You can use your opening sentences to establish a rapport with the audience and possibly overcome any prejudices which they may have towards you, as this speaker did: 'Like you, I have not been to university but I have done every job in this factory, so you can be sure I'm not going to suggest any changes that won't work.' By reaching out towards the audience, the speaker was helping them to accept his proposals.

Direction – give them a route map

Tell your audience what you are going to say, say it and then tell them you've said it. The audience wants to know what's coming and it will make it easier for them to follow your talk if you share your map with them. It's not necessary to be very formal in this, as you will see from this extract from a warehouse manager's talk: 'I have two suggestions that I hope will show you how we can improve the layout of our stores department.' A distribution manager chose to preface her talk like this: 'The problem of incorrect deliveries has to be tackled in three ways. One, why do they occur? Two, what can we do to stop them? And three, how much will it cost?'

Alan's presentation

Here are the four opening sentences of Alan's presentation to the Board:

'Junior staff are costing this company five times as much as our competitors. Why? Because none of them are staying more than six months and some are leaving after only a few weeks.' (Attention getter)

'I'm going to suggest how we can reduce that cost and increase our efficiency.' (Benefits)

'During the last month I've talked to every department manager as well as many personnel managers outside the company, so I think I know what will work for us and what won't.' (Credentials)

'I want to cover four areas. First I'd like to look at how this problem has developed, second how much it costs us, third why staff don't stay longer, and fourth what we can do about it.' (Direction)

Closing Sentences

Your listeners' attention will always be at its highest at the beginning and at the end of your talk, so you must take advantage of this and conclude with a positive restatement of your message. You will sometimes see an apparently confident speaker suddenly mutter a quick thank you and sit down abruptly. This gives the impression that the speaker can't wait to finish what was an unpleasant experience. There is no need to thank the audience and often these words are only used to help the speaker get off the stage and out of the limelight.

Your conclusion shouldn't come as a surprise. It should be predictable in order to allow the audience to pay maximum attention. It should be brief and not include any new material.

Below are listed some of the ways in which you can end decisively.

Summarise

Use phrases like 'in conclusion', 'to sum up' or 'finally', to indicate that you are about to finish. Be sure to end shortly after these words – don't continue for another 5 minutes.

Ask for action

You can summarise and tell the audience what you expect them to do: 'I think you'll agree, having heard what I've said, that we must increase the budget for this project. Therefore I am asking you to vote for the increase.'

Ask a question

You may want to leave the audience with a question. This is particularly effective when you have posed a problem and have offered a solution: 'The question is not whether we can afford to increase our budget but whether we can afford *not* to. The decision is with you; what do you think?'

Use a quotation

Once again a good book of quotations will provide an ending that is humorous or profound, depending on the mood you want to create: 'Lord Mancroft once said that a speech is like a love affair. Any fool can start it, but to end it requires considerable skill.'

Tell an anecdote

A story told at the end of a talk must be short and emphasise the main theme of what you have been stressing. Remember to personalise it and make it relevant to your audience. After a recent talk on career development to a group of women managers I told them this story: 'Women are in a stronger position than ever before – even my young nephew has recognised this. He came home recently and told his father that he was second in class. First place was held by a girl. "Surely you're not going to be beaten by a mere girl," said his father. "Well you see," said my nephew, "girls are not as mere as they used to be."'

Alan's presentation

Alan ended his presentation by summarising his recommendation and asking for action:

'So in conclusion I recommend we stop spending unnecessary time and money taking on staff who are unsuitable and who leave after a short time. We need a trained personnel officer. I would like to have your permission to advertise for a personnel officer. In the long run this will cost us less and help to create a happier workforce which will lead to increased productivity and efficiency.'

SUMMARY

- Select a suitable structure, add signposts and mini summaries.

- Expand your key ideas with supporting evidence.

- Add colour to the grey patches using relevant examples and personal illustrations.

- Choose a punchy beginning.

- End decisively.

4

How to Hold an Audience

'Speak properly and in as few words as you can,
but always plainly, for the end of speech is not ostentation,
but to be understood'
WILLIAM PENN

Listeners Are Not Readers

Before I suggest some techniques on how to hold your audience's attention, I'd like to revisit the main differences between
reading and listening to be aware of if you are going to be able
to write and deliver a convincing and natural presentation.

I have already described the problems of keeping the attention of your listeners with the spoken word. *Listening is not
easy*. The listener's thoughts provide a plethora of distractions.
Reading is different; a reader who is distracted rereads a
sentence or paragraph or even an entire chapter. On the first
day of a holiday have you had the experience of repeatedly re-
reading the opening chapter of your book? You couldn't
concentrate because your thoughts kept returning to the work
you had left behind and the possible problems that might have
occurred during your absence. However, if your mind

wandered, you could return to your book and attempt to concentrate again. Listeners can't do this. If they don't concentrate during your talk, they don't have an opportunity of relistening. They only have *one chance to understand* what you are saying.

Readers can vary the speed of their reading and, if the material is complex or unfamiliar, they can stop and refer to a dictionary or even discuss it with a colleague. Listeners *can't vary the pace* of the speaker's delivery.

Readers can skim-read in order to see the total idea and re-read what they feel is relevant. Listeners *can't anticipate your total talk*; only you know the complete picture, and therefore what might seem clear to you may be incomprehensible to your listeners.

So, because listeners can't move backwards or forwards, nor vary the speed of their listening, what can you do to help them to follow, understand and retain what you are saying?

Tell Them What to Expect

If you give your listeners an outline of your talk or a map to show them where you intend leading them, they will find it easier to follow you. This is the equivalent of the reader who skim-reads to identify the main points before settling down to read the detail. Here is how one speaker identified the path along which she was taking her listeners: 'There are three main areas that the marketing department has examined over the past six months. These are advertising, pricing and sales. During my talk, I am going to look at each of these in turn. Firstly, advertising . . .'

Tell Them Where You Are

You can also help your listeners by summarising and recapping so that they know how far along the path you have progressed.

Here is an example from the same speech: 'So, to summarise our two main recommendations on advertising, we recommend (a) more consumer advertising and (b) limited but clearly defined trade advertising. So much for our recommendations for the first area that we looked at – advertising. [pause] Now I'd like to turn to the second area – pricing.' You'll notice from this example that the speaker has numbered each of her points.

In her final summary, she looked back and told the listeners what they had heard – this is the equivalent of the reader re-reading to ensure he has understood: 'So the three areas the marketing department examined were advertising, pricing and sales and we are making the following three recommendations. Firstly, for advertising, we recommend more consumer advertising and limited but clearly defined advertisements for the trade. Second, on pricing, we recommend a new and simplified discount structure and, finally, on sales, we recommend a two-tier sales force.'

In the written form, these recaps and summaries appear repetitious and even unnecessary, but remember they are not for the eye, they are for the ear. Listeners need these reinforcements to help them follow you as well as to help them retain what you are saying; without them, it is like trying to read a book with no paragraphs or chapters.

Gather Up Your Stragglers

You know that listeners are not concentrating consistently so you must gather them up as you progress along your path. *Rhetorical questions* are an excellent method of attracting listeners back from their mental undergrowth. You might ask, 'So how do these new plans affect you in the sales department?' or 'Why am I telling you about the changes in our budget forecasting?'

Listeners will concentrate on your answer because you have

involved them with a rhetorical question and you have also indicated what is coming next. Use rhetorical questions throughout your script – they are powerful attention grabbers and signposts to what is to follow.

You can also *anticipate your audience's reaction* by saying: 'You may be asking yourself, "So what on earth has this got to do with the sales department?" or you may be wondering how much extra all these improvements are going to cost.'

With this technique, you are anticipating that your listeners are about to wander off your path into their mental under-growth and you are enticing them back before they can stray too far.

Remember to *recap constantly* as you progress from one point to another; this will help people who have disappeared down Route 350 and may have lost the thread of your argu-ment. Their own thoughts are continually interrupting their concentration and you need to help them follow the logic of your talk by signposting each point and recapping frequently. One speaker, who was presenting a problem/solution structure to her staff group, used a combination of recapping and rhetor-ical questions to help her audience follow her talk: 'I told you I would be tackling the problem of our lack of expansion from two angles: the shortage of available funds and overstocking of merchandise. First, I've given you the details of our current financial situation. You may be wondering what these figures really mean. I can best answer that by referring to my second point – overstocking. Why have we got a warehouse full of navy blue suits? Let me tell you . . .'

In this example the speaker has reminded the audience that she will be tackling the problem from two angles; she tells them that she has already given details of the first point, raises their awareness of what she is talking about with a rhetorical question and announces the second point she is going to discuss.

Appeal to the Emotions

Facts and information on their own won't change anyone's mind. You must show *why* your ideas will benefit the listeners. This is where probing questions in advance of the meeting pay off. You know what sort of people you are facing. You have assessed what makes them tick. Simply convert your facts into advantages for them. Demonstrate how your solution can solve their problem. Explain how you can cater for their needs. Be sure to describe advantages that are relevant to *them*.

Here are a few examples of facts followed by advantages:

- This is a book on effective speaking (fact). Reading it will help you to present your ideas in a convincing manner (advantage).

- It is a short book (fact). Therefore it's easy to carry and you can read it anywhere (advantage).

- It is reasonably priced (fact). You can become a more effective speaker than your colleagues for a small outlay (advantage).

Another interesting example of facts and advantages or features and benefits was described to me by a fellow trainer. She said, 'You don't sell the drill, you sell the holes.' No one buys a drill because it has the most impressive features, you buy a drill because of its ability to make holes.

In order to convert facts or information into an advantage for your listeners, you must ask yourself what these facts or information will do for them. What benefit will this provide? What need will this satisfy? Your listeners will not buy ideas unless they recognise that they have a problem your ideas will solve. But, once having seen the need, they will be more receptive to the advantages and benefits of your ideas, provided they satisfy that need. They may be uninterested in the facts and only interested in the advantages that they provide. You may choose to begin by showing the benefits that appeal to their emotions and follow them with a logical description of the facts. Changes of attitude and decision making can depend as much on an emotional response as on rational arguments.

Make It Easy for Them to Agree

Don't expect to convert your listeners to your views instantly. No one likes to admit that they are wrong, so make it easy for them. Encourage them to contribute by allowing them to acknowledge some of the benefits. Persuasion is often achieved by letting the listeners talk themselves into accepting your point of view. Sometimes you can smooth the path for them by revealing that you used to share their point of view. You can tell your audience how a particular advantage convinced you to change your mind. In this way they keep their self-esteem while agreeing with you. Your aim is to persuade your listeners to adopt your ideas, without causing them to feel that they are 'wrong' and that you are 'right'.

With practice, you will be able to convince listeners that your solution was really theirs. Counsellors learn the art of non-judgemental listening until their clients work out their own problems. You may need to push and prod your listener towards your selected goal, but it's surprising how often people will adopt new ideas with little resistance, providing they feel that they haven't been forced into it. So steer clear of the hard sell.

Ask for Commitment

Make sure that your listeners are committed to your ideas and, if necessary, that an agreement is reached on the action that should follow, for example, 'So we are agreed that we'll keep the front office open between Christmas and the New Year but the factory will be closed during that period. How shall we announce this decision?' Once a commitment has been made, steer clear of any further discussion and refrain from looking triumphant.

A Convincing Delivery

To convince and persuade successfully you must have personal commitment. You must believe in your cause and be able to show that you do. A nonchalant, unemotional presentation will fail. You must be able to *show enthusiasm*. It's not enough to feel it, you must display your heart on your face and in your voice. You can't simply read out a script and hope to express heartfelt emotion. Your emotions should be part of you. Reading a script under these circumstances suggests that you are not being honest. You need eye contact to demonstrate sincerity. Remember that the impact of your words will be diminished by poor body language. In fact, if your words say one thing and your body another, you run the risk of appearing hypocritical and deceitful.

Don't allow yourself to be interrupted or distracted by comments from other members of the group. Don't allow your voice to drop at the end of each sentence. Make sure you have sufficient breath in your lungs to carry your voice to the end.

Try to match your body language to that of your audience. Students of body language have discovered that people who feel at ease with one another tend, unconsciously, to sit or stand in a similar fashion and to change their position to match each other. You can observe this in restaurants or in public lounges or even at office meetings. Those who are in agreement will be sitting in a similar manner. The dissenter will be leaning back or forwards to demonstrate his disagreement physically. We naturally follow this 'mirroring' of those with whom we feel comfortable, without even being aware of it. To create a harmonious atmosphere for your persuasion, try to ensure that your body language doesn't conflict with that of your listeners. For example, if your listener is sitting and you are standing as you try to convince him that he should work over the weekend, your chances of success will be improved if you place yourself at his level. All your communication should be face to face. You are not seeking to intimidate or force your listeners to accept your views, so aim to balance your body language with theirs.

The adage that 'People buy people first' holds true. Often your listeners will not be assessing the value of your ideas. They will be judging *you*. If they like you, they'll want to believe in you and your opinions, even when they can find no logical reason for doing so. Appealing to people's emotions makes a lot of sense, provided that this doesn't result in them feeling manipulated.

Involving Techniques

However passionate a speaker you are, if you talk at your listeners continuously you won't convince or persuade them. They are likely to escape down Route 350. Remember, they may want to make a point, ask a question or even agree with you! Schedule *pauses* into your presentation so that you can invite your listeners to contribute: 'Can you see how this new schedule would ease your workload?', 'How do you feel this could fit into your existing budget?' or 'How does this sound to you?'

Vary the words you use to appeal to your listeners' senses. Some people can '*feel* an idea', while others want to '*hear* how it sounds' or '*see* how it's going to work'. You can identify from their conversation which category of words is most comfortable for them.

How Else Can You Help the Audience to Listen?

Facts on their own tend to be dull and you will need to translate them into *visual word pictures*: 'Our warehouse handled twenty tons of merchandise this year. That's about equivalent to a row of eight terraced houses' or 'Our representatives travelled over 80,000 miles each this year; that's like going to Manchester from London 400 times.'

Try to illustrate with *personal examples*. This speaker was describing the drawbacks of being self-employed: 'Many people envy me because I work from home, but you know I never get away from my "office" and I find myself opening business letters even on a Saturday morning.'

Nothing helps an audience understand as well as *personal stories*. I remember seeing a very successful sales rep graphically telling an audience about her first disastrous sales call and how she had gone home and nearly given up on the spot. It was her own story and all the audience shared her feelings of rejection and admired her determination to carry on.

The audience will always warm to you if you can reveal your own feelings and weaknesses. It can be difficult to do so. For this reason, the audience will respect your courage. Early on in my training career, I remember making a remark towards the end of a day's training to the effect that I had felt nervous at the start of the day. I was amazed at the number of people who were reassured by this comment and pleased that I was prepared to make it to them. On reflection I realised that it was because I had felt comfortable with the group that I was able to describe my feelings. If you build in a few *self-revealing sentences*, your audience will feel you are treating them as friends.

Use personal anecdotes to support your arguments. If you have experiences that illustrate your main point, the audience will understand and remember them more easily.

Use Relevant Illustrations

Make sure your anecdotes or examples are relevant to your audience. I heard a successful talk to a group of schoolboys by a management consultant, in which he compared management with being the captain of a cricket team, matching and balancing the strengths and personalities of the players. On another occasion a politician was discussing government revenue and expenditure in terms of billions of pounds; this could be difficult to comprehend for some people, until he equated it to the wages and bills that are familiar to every householder: 'Some bills have to be paid every week while others can be paid every month – but you have to make sure you save a bit every week to pay them.' The amounts may be larger but the principles are the same.

In a sales presentation, you may want to paint a word picture of how your client will feel if she buys your product, by describing a similar situation with another client: 'He told me he felt a great sense of relief after the new coffee machine was installed – no more rows about whose turn it was to make coffee.'

The majority of road accidents happen within five miles of the home: just another boring statistic until a doctor friend of mine told me that if he hadn't been wearing his seatbelt, he wouldn't be alive today. He had popped out to buy a newspaper and had had a bad accident.

I have heard a sales manager, who appeared to be remote from the problems of his representatives, vividly describing the times when he was in direct selling and was required to achieve impossible targets set by his manager. His stories were relevant to the audience and illustrated many of the points in his talk.

Appealing to the Listener

If you want to be persuasive, put yourself in your listeners' shoes and ask yourself how you can help them to follow your talk and what will make it relevant to them.

Some speakers like to follow the FEB technique:

Feature or Fact
Effect of the F
Benefit to the listener

This technique is applied in the following way: 'Because [feature], you will be able to [effect] which means that [benefit].' For example, '*Because* we have expanded the car park, *you will always be able to* park, *which means that* you will save time in the morning.'

These words 'because', 'you will be able to', and 'which means that', are only intended as guides and you can choose your own phrases to fit the sense of your sentence. Here's another example: 'As the Board has accepted this proposal, you can start work immediately and say goodbye to your money problems.'

As you prepare your talk, imagine that you have to answer listeners who are asking 'So what? What does this mean? How does this affect me, my company, my department, my situation?' You should be able to answer those questions with FEB.

Talking Numbers

In general, you should avoid speaking numbers. They are difficult to grasp by ear and can be confusing. Unless precision is essential, round up figures so that the listeners can identify them more easily, e.g. say 'nearly half' instead of '48.27 per cent' or 'just over three-quarters' instead of '76.92 per cent'. Work out a method of showing a measurement so that it means more to the audience: 'From earth to the moon is 240,250 miles. That means that driving a family car for 10 hours a day at 50 miles per hour, you would arrive there in 16 months, that is on 11th May next year.'

If your talk must include figures, consider using a visual aid or handout so that your listeners can follow your reasoning more easily.

Size

Size is also difficult to visualise unless you compare it with a familiar object, such as, smaller than a matchbox; about the size of two double-decker buses; as high as that ceiling; or as long as this room.

Avoid Jargon and Abbreviations

Beware of speaking in terms that are unfamiliar to your audience – this can be very distracting and can cause many of your listeners to switch their energy to pondering on the meaning of a phrase or an abbreviation and so lose the thread of your argument.

Some terminology or abbreviations, which are part of your everyday vocabulary when talking to colleagues, could be misleading or even incomprehensible to many people. Carefully trim these distractions from your talk. Explain abbreviations at the beginning of your talk. If you feel you must use shorthand because the unabbreviated names are too long, remember to include the full name from time to time.

Convenient Clichés or Piquant Prose

This is an important point because speakers can often be unaware that they habitually use imprecise words and hackneyed phrases that are boring to the listener. Here is an example of what I mean:

I'm absolutely delighted that so many of you could come here tonight as it's raining cats and dogs outside, but at least it's warm and snug in here. I've been asked to speak to you tonight and I don't mind telling you that I'm a bundle of nerves and I hope I haven't bitten off more than I can chew.

I know I can depend on your support so I won't mince matters. Let's face it, things often get worse before they get better. So, not to put too fine a point on it, I'm going to ask you to stick it out. From the bottom of my heart, I appeal to you to put yourselves in my shoes at this point in time. Is this a fate worse than death? I can safely say I think it is, so without further ado, I'll leave you with this thought as I beat a hasty retreat, better safe than sorry.

Of course no one would include so many clichés but it's often easier to use a familiar phrase than to find a more original expression. Try to avoid clichés that have ceased to have an impact – if you don't, your listeners will find you uninspiring and may eventually stop listening. It takes time to be creative and imaginative, but if you invest in a dictionary of synonyms you'll find that your speech will become livelier and more entertaining.

SUMMARY

- Announce the structure, i.e. share your route map.

- Summarise and recap frequently, i.e. how far you've travelled and where you've been.

- Identify each point clearly, i.e. indicate the landmarks of your journey.

- Use rhetorical questions to regain the audience's attention, i.e. give them signposts.

- Use examples, personal stories and anecdotes that are relevant to the audience to illustrate your ideas, i.e. describe the beauty spots.

- Avoid jargon and abbreviations, i.e. avoid foreign language.

- Summarise the main points and, if necessary, ask for action before you conclude, i.e. recall the landmarks.

5

How to Design Visual Aids

'Every picture tells a story'

advertising slogan for Sloane's backache and kidney pills, circa 1907

Visual aids, properly used, are an effective way to hold your audience's attention. This chapter will explain the advantages and disadvantages of the most commonly used visual aids, as well as describe how to design and make visuals that will enhance your talk or presentation. In Chapter 6 you will find hints on using visual aid equipment.

Adding Audience Value

The objective of most business presentations is to inform or persuade, or a combination of both, but information received by listening is retained for less time than that which is received by seeing. This means that visual aids help to make your talk memorable. They also help to explain complex ideas in a form that is easily understood; relationships and comparisons can be shown more clearly in a visual format; statistics, figures and financial data in general are more digestible and comprehensible when presented visually.

Visuals can reinforce an idea that you have already discussed in words; for instance you could outline a cost-saving theory and then show visually what the actual savings would be in practice.

Avoiding Aid Dependency

Speakers often regard visuals as the magic ingredient that will turn a turgid talk into a professional presentation. In fact I have seen more good talks ruined by inappropriate visuals than I have seen poor talks improved by good ones. Even when the visuals are good, the speaker often finds it difficult to incorporate them smoothly so that they, and the speaker's behaviour, only distract the audience. So make sure your visual is *an aid* and not a distraction, and make sure your aid is *visual.*

Beware of adding visuals to your presentation for the wrong reasons; they can take time, be difficult to use and confuse the audience. Many speakers I know use them as a prompt. They have most of their presentation on slides and refer to them throughout their talk. This is an insult to the audience! Such speakers are ignoring all the advantages of talking to a live audience and suffering all the disadvantages of reading. Your audience can be reminded of your key points after you have spoken them, so use a visual to summarise but not as a prompt.

Don't use visuals to brighten up an uninteresting talk – improve your talk and only use a visual to illustrate it more vividly. Also don't be tempted to add visuals because the other speakers are doing so. Your talk may not need them. In some organisations, if you arrive at a meeting without visuals you are judged to be ill-prepared. It can be difficult to go against a strong corporate culture; however, you could reduce the number of visuals and improve your delivery so that people look and listen to *you*. Wean them and yourself off visual aid dependency. Instead use visuals to:

- present facts, concepts, figures, in a comparative or structured form;

- aid comprehension and prevent misunderstanding;

- reinforce your message;

- focus your listeners' attention;

- maintain interest and help retention;

- motivate the audience to make a decision;

- add humour and spice.

Non-negotiable Visual Aids

There are some situations where visual aids are essential. The first is to show an idea visually. On page 24 you will see a sketch of a mind map. This concept is also described in the text of Chapter 2 Preparing and Planning a Presentation, but I think you'll agree that by seeing an example it is easier to understand. Any discussion of techniques or methods can benefit from a visual illustrating how they work in practice. Cut-away drawings of machinery or tools can be very helpful on practical, instructional courses. I have heard that you can always recognise an MBA graduate because they can't resist drawing business models! Nevertheless, this is another example of how a visual aid adds value to an idea.

Figures are difficult to understand when spoken. Comparisons can be made more easily when they are displayed visually. Here is a pie chart showing the relative importance of three factors to consider when speaking. These figures have already appeared in the text of Chapter 1 What is Communication?, but I think you'll agree they make more impression when portrayed as shown in the illustration.

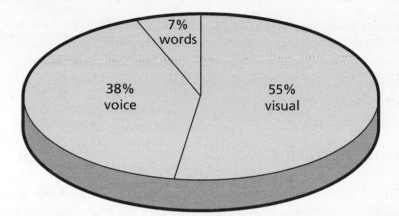

Speakers' impact

Considerations for Visual Aids

Once you have decided that your talk would benefit from the inclusion of some visual material, choosing how to display it can be difficult. The table below (see pages 65–7) shows the advantages and disadvantages of the various types of visual aid and you'll see that not one of them is perfect. However, here are some of the considerations for you to bear in mind, when selecting a visual style.

Available equipment

Most companies have either a data projector or an overhead projector and flip chart, but if you are presenting a talk off site, check the specifications of the data projector. Audio-visual equipment is available to hire in most large cities, but if you are using hired equipment, don't try to save money by only ordering it for the day of your talk. Make sure you can rehearse with it at least one day in advance and, for more complex presentations with several speakers, ensure that you have it for two or three days before the actual presentation. Hotel equipment varies from excellent to appalling, so make sure you see it beforehand in order to check its suitability for your talk. I have run courses throughout the UK and am amazed that some hotels offering 'Conference Facilities' can be so unaware of what is needed by speakers.

Size of audience

If the audience can't see what's on the visual, you are likely to antagonise them and lose their attention. Certain aids aren't suitable for groups of more than 25 people, i.e. flip chart, blackboard, whiteboard. This is a rough estimate, and the size and layout of the room may allow you to increase or decrease that number. If you are presenting to a small group of five or six people, don't dismiss the idea of visuals as inappropriate; a large screen is not always necessary as you can easily project on to a blank wall.

Size and layout of room

Long, narrow rooms with poor lighting are not suitable for the smaller aids such as flip charts. Sometimes conference facilities offered by older hotels are located in rooms with pillars or asymmetric walls that can make it difficult to set up a screen which is visible to all the audience. If you are sitting on a platform you may have to rearrange the speakers' chairs so that they don't obstruct the screen.

Lighting

You may have to darken the room. Some offices don't have blinds at the windows and I have come across hotel rooms with curtains that are decorative but not functional. Overhead projector slides can be shown in natural light, but occasionally you will need to block out sunlight if it is shining directly on to the screen. Also, 35mm and low power data projectors need dimmed lights. Avoid shadows on the flip chart if possible and don't place it against a window or another source of bright light as this will make it difficult to read.

Seating arrangements

Make sure you arrange the seating so that everyone has a clear view of the screen. In the seating diagrams on pages 214–15 you will see that the position of the projector and screen can usually be adjusted so that it's visible to everyone.

Cost versus frequency of use

Slides can be made easily in the office, but for sales presentations to clients or large conferences, consider using a production company. If you are using the slides repeatedly, i.e. a road show travelling round the country or for training and teaching purposes, it's worth the extra expense to have them professionally produced.

Visual aids

Advantages	*Disadvantages*
Blackboards	
No mechanisms to go wrong; flexible; mistakes easily corrected; can be quickly erased	Chalk is messy to use; creates a classroom atmosphere; difficult to erase well if old; suitable for small groups only; not portable

Advantages	*Disadvantages*
Whiteboards	
Similar advantages to blackboards; also presentation clearer with special pens; easy and cleaner to use	Limited to small groups; generally only available in training rooms; not portable
Flip chart	
Easy to use; not much can go wrong; readily available; cheap; versatile – can be used pre-written or constructed during the course of the talk; portable	Can be difficult to write on quickly; only suitable for small audience of less than 25
Overhead projectors	
Transparencies easily and economically produced on PowerPoint; flexible; possible to change order or omit slides during presentation; build up of information possible with several slides; screen is bright and clear in normal room light; suitable for small or large audiences; can be used like the flip chart with a continuous roll of acetate so that the speaker can write calculations or notes on to it	Can break down or suffer bulb failure, usually fan cooled so produces background noise that can be distracting; must be constantly switched on and off so as not to leave irrelevant material or a blank screen showing; speaker has to be careful not to obscure audience's view of the screen with the projector
Laptops/Data projectors	
Have all the advantages of overhead projector and 35mm slides; available to most presenters; smooth transitions between slides; looks professional; use of special effects and sound adds impact and interest; can check visual by looking at laptop, not over shoulder to screen	Maximum of two people can see laptop screen so usually a data projector is required; extended set-up time and technical failure can reflect badly on the presenter; presenter can be tied to laptop unless remote control is used; colour on PC may change when projected

Advantages	*Disadvantages*
Video Clips	
Can be incorporated into laptop presentation or played on monitors; adds movement and external presenters	Sound reproduction on laptop can be low quality so use external speakers; use sparingly or the video will dominate your presentation
35mm slides	
Very sharp, bright image; focuses attention of audience; wide variety of material can be shown; easily stored and carried; projectors readily available; fast and smooth operation; suits any size audience; useful for more formal method of presentation	Low light makes it difficult for audience to make notes and for the speaker to maintain eye contact; less flexible than overhead projector; cannot change order or omit slides; artwork can be expensive; largely replaced by data projectors
Physical objects	
Can save a lot of unnecessary description; ensures everyone has uniform idea of what speaker is talking about; members of the audience can handle them – direct contact is always useful; versatile; models; objects and props often easily available.	Passing round objects is time-consuming and distracting; small groups only, holding up article unsuitable for small objects or large audiences; models can be expensive to prepare.

How to Design Effective Visuals

Most of what I'm including in this section applies to slides, however, some of the basic rules regarding simplicity and clarity are also applicable to prepared flip charts. Even if you have an in-house audio visual department or if you intend to use an outside agency, as a speaker, you should have a good idea of what makes a successful visual, as they will need to follow your instructions.

Avoid verbal visuals

As we know, a picture is worth a thousand words. Unfortunately, in many of the presentations I see, a thousand words have been put on the visual aid.

Words don't make good visuals, but many speakers consider that their listeners will be unable to follow a talk without a script in front of them. The greatest insult of all is to start your presentation with a visual proclaiming 'Good Morning' or 'Sales Presentation for . . .' These words should be spoken, not written. Words on a visual encourage your listeners to become readers and while they are readers, they can't be listeners.

Verbal visuals are a distraction as members of your audience will be reading at different speeds and if you attempt to read the slide for them, most of them will have finished before you anyway.

Bullet point slides should be limited to five words per point and five points per slide. Avoid adding numbers at the beginning and full stops at the end of each line. The points should be brief and punchy phrases, not full sentences or even, perish the thought, paragraphs. The only exception I would make to this recommendation is when you are talking to overseas audiences whose knowledge of English may be variable. In this case, word slides can help them follow your presentation more easily. This is particularly true of Japanese audiences. For more, see Chapter 20 Virtual and Cross-cultural Meetings.

Remember that word slides can be made more interesting by using text shadow, backgrounds and shapes. Reveal your bullet points one by one by using PowerPoint transitions and build up slides (see below for more on this), or a mask on OHPs.

Any words included on your visuals must be legible from the seats furthest from the screen. Use a uniform typeface, and upper and lower case throughout, and always write words horizontally, even in pie charts or when identifying machinery parts that may be positioned at an angle. Add bold or italics to highlight key words.

It is a simple matter to add pictures to your visuals by using a scanner or digital camera. I was struck by how quickly this equipment has become part of mainstream business life when I sold my house. Two years ago an estate agent simply measured the rooms and gave prospective buyers a brief description. Today she takes several colour photographs that are printed with the house details and distributed within hours or accessed through a website.

Keep them simple

The Microsoft visual aids package, PowerPoint, offers a wealth of special effects and it's tempting to use all those fancy borders and elaborate templates. Resist the temptation. Choose the simple background that will enhance, not obscure, your message, and avoid adding logos and slide headings that significantly reduce the usable area of your visual. Many visuals are ineffective because they are complicated and contain too much information. They are difficult to understand and therefore become a distraction. You may need to separate out material in order to present it on several slides; analyse what is the most significant data and reject the rest.

Remember that round figures are easier to understand, i.e. £1 million is more comprehensible than £1,103,284.83. If you are preparing a series of slides showing the information in stages, you could, for example, start with a graph showing the sales targets and add the actual sales figures; with the build-up technique you can add information to each slide; for instance, a map of Great Britain could be filled in with regional sales figures. This method allows you to remain in control of the speed at which your audience assimilates information and also allows you to explain any inconsistencies or anomalies in the data. For example, the sales manager might say, 'You will notice that sales figures for Scotland appear to have increased at a faster rate than those for the rest of the country, but bear in mind that International Mechanics, one of our larger customers, moved to Aberdeen in January and so their sales are included in Scotland now.'

Tables of figures rarely make good visuals, as they often contain too much information and they are difficult to read. Pie charts and bar charts can be a simpler method for relaying that kind of data.

Keep them uniform

I have found that clients who previously considered a few typed notes on acetate to be an adequate visual aid will sometimes go to the opposite extreme after some tuition on the merits of creative visuals and use the flip chart extensively, in between showing a PowerPoint slide show, with video and sound effects. Don't use too many types of visual and don't attempt to make them too diverse. A jumble of typefaces and styles and a mixture of colours gives the impression that both speaker and company are disorganised and confused. Choose a clear, simple font like Arial or a classic font like Times New Roman, and a type size no smaller than 28 point, and use it throughout your slides with a bold background colour to create a smart effect. Maintain a consistent style throughout for borders, headings and company logo position. If you are using transitions, ensure they are uniform and only use the special effects sparingly for impact.

Transitions and builds

Transitions and builds are the movement from one slide to the next, or the build-up of text or images on to or away from the visual aid. They can be used when projecting from a laptop.

Just because they are available do not be tempted to experiment with every one of them. Your selection should reflect the overall atmosphere and key messages you wish to put across.

For informal presentations, such as internal department meetings or training sessions, use two or three of the following transitions: fly from left, wipe right, box in and out, blinds and chequer-board.

For more formal audiences, such as clients, senior executives and shareholders, you could also use fly from left and wipe right as a safe transition, as well as dissolve between messages. Use cuts to highlight sub-messages. Add boxes in and out to vary your transitions.

For a more upbeat audience such as a sales conference, all the above are suitable, plus a fade through black to provide a complete change of scene. Flying points in from the top is also effective. For special interest use the split vertical out (curtain opening) to open and split vertical in (curtain closing) to end.

I recently saw a key message being pulled in by a sports car which stopped with a squeal of brakes. As this was the only 'special effect' in an otherwise serious presentation, it had impact. But I did notice that the discussion after the presentation seemed to centre on 'How did he do that trick with the car?' rather than the key message! This is always a danger with unusual effects.

Beware of using Clip Art as many people find it hackneyed and it seldom adds real value to the visual. However, you can modify and enhance standard Clip Art by using the Draw command so that it is personalised for your presentation.

Keep them colourful

Judicial use of colour can significantly enhance your visuals, as you can use it as a background or to highlight important data, to underline and for bullet points and arrows. Aim for a contrast, for instance light letters on a dark background. If you are not confident about your colour sense use a colour wheel to guide you as to which colours complement each other.

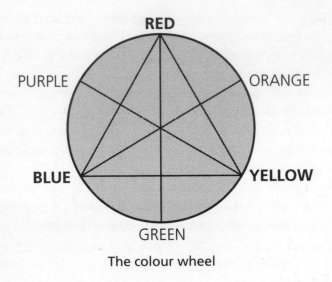

The colour wheel

If you want vibrant colours use the ones from opposite sides, for example, orange and blue or yellow and purple. An image stands out strongly when a warm colour is combined with a cool colour. A common example of this is yellow lettering on a blue background.

However, some colours change or lose their intensity when they are projected. Always avoid white letters on a yellow background or vice versa and pink on red, as they become invisible. You can use a primary background colour to indicate the various sections of your talk, i.e. the sales manager could use blue on the slides when illustrating her section on key accounts, and change to red when she moved on to new business. Avoid combinations of green and red, as these will be indistinguishable to people who are colour-blind. The key to using colour successfully is to keep it simple.

Keep them humorous

If you can introduce an element of humour into a serious presentation, you will be revealing the fun side of your character and this will warm your audience to you. Beware of being flippant, but you can add a light touch to dry material to help maintain your listeners' interest. For example, bar charts can depict your product. If you sell cars show your sales as bars shaped like vehicles.

Make your actual bullet point more interesting. Replace the standard dot or square with a symbol such as a pointing finger, a star or a representation of your key message, e.g. £££ or $$$ for increased revenue. Refer to the font options in PowerPoint under Wingdings for ideas.

Don't forget to double check all visuals for typos and spelling mistakes *before* you show them to an audience.

Visual styles

Pie charts

A pie chart is a circle divided into 'slices', which visually indicates the relative value of each slice to the whole (see illustration at the beginning of this chapter). It is a very useful type of visual as it's easy to produce and suitable for both technical and non-technical audiences. Use as few sectors as possible and never exceed five or six. The most important sector should be placed at the 12 o'clock position and arrange the other components from the smallest to the largest or vice versa.

Sectors can be coloured or highlighted to indicate their importance but be sure that any lettering or figures will show up over the background colour. Sometimes it's preferable to identify the sectors by means of arrows positioned at the side of the pie. Remember always to place your words horizontally; don't follow the shape of the pie.

Bar charts

Pie charts are useful to compare fractions within a single whole, but bar charts can be used to highlight the relationship between two variables, e.g. age and salary, or productivity in geographical areas, as well as to illustrate trends and make comparisons. They should be simple and easy to follow, so when designing them, you must identify the relevant information and discard the rest, or present it as a second or third visual.

Bar charts can be drawn vertically or horizontally, but the former are more appropriate to indicate a time element and when one item has to be shown several times, e.g. annual sales figures for the last five years. The timescale is normally shown along the bottom line.

Horizontal bar charts have two advantages: first, the information can be presented in any sequence, e.g. sales figures for the month of July can be shown alphabetically by the rep's name, or by geographical area, or in order of size, or even randomly; secondly, there is more space to identify each bar. Remember that the labels can be placed at either end of each bar or even below and above them.

Sliding bar charts are used to show a sub-division within a total, e.g. each bar showing sales figures could be sub-divided into sales for existing customers and sales from new customers. Using different colours for each division gives them more impact.

Line charts and graphs

These can be used instead of vertical bar charts and are particularly useful when a greater number of time periods needs to be illustrated; for instance, a three-year sales period with monthly totals would require 36 bars which would be difficult to represent clearly. Line charts or graphs are also useful to illustrate minor variations in data, which would not be noticeable with bar charts. Variations can be highlighted by using a broken scale that does not begin at zero, but with the amount where the minor variation appears; e.g. if the monthly sales figures over a twelve-month period ranged between £140,000 and £145,000 per month, the scale ranges from £135,000 to £155,000 in order to emphasise the variations. Be sure that the broken scale is clearly marked, otherwise the audience will assume that it starts at zero.

Flow and organisation charts

Flow charts illustrate the stages of development in a process or the passage of documents through a system, and organisation charts show the functional relationships and flow within a group or company. Both are useful to demonstrate visually links and connections that might be difficult to understand and remember without a chart (see overleaf).

They can also be used to demonstrate visually the structure of your talk. Throughout your presentation, you can refer back to the organisation chart as a reminder to the audience of the structure and progress of your key points.

Tables of figures

These should be interpreted in a visual manner. However, if due to budgeting or time constraints this isn't possible, consider highlighting the key figures, so that the audience concentrates on it immediately and doesn't get drawn into reading the rest of the table. Block out the irrelevant information if you can. Remember that the figures on their own are insignificant without analysis, so don't leave the audience to puzzle over their meaning. Don't use the following on your visual:

- computer printouts;

- typewritten material;

A flow chart showing the progress of mail through an office

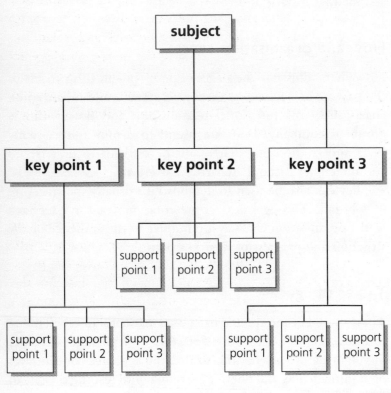

Organisational chart

- tables of figures;

- forms;

- printed material from books, newspapers, articles.

Financial and technical presentations often suffer from too much detail. This is particularly noticeable when expert speakers are addressing lay audiences. If you are in this position, make sure that your audience research is thorough, enabling you to put yourself in their shoes. Stand back and isolate the most important features, and ignore the qualifying elements that may be fascinating to you because you are so closely involved with the subject. Aim to make your visuals simple and uncluttered by detail; show the audience the benefits to them of your argument, not the technical background.

Be Original

So far, this chapter has been devoted to the traditional methods of adding a visual element to your talk. But don't limit yourself. Be original. I saw a stimulating use of some very ordinary props by a chairman during a presentation to his staff on the company's gross profit. He opened with: '£20 million sounds a lot of money, but what happens to it?' He proceeded to take a jug of orange juice and poured it into a number of glasses that he had set up on the table. 'So much has to go on wages and salaries,' he said, filling up one glass. 'We must allow this much for National Insurance Contributions and PAYE,' he said, as he moved on to the next glass. He proceeded to fill the rest of the glasses (he had marked the correct level for each one before he began his talk) with the overheads of the company. Eventually, he was left with a small amount of orange juice in the jug. 'This is what's left,' he said and measured it into the remaining two glasses. 'Just enough to pay Corporation Tax and dividends to the shareholders.' He held up the empty jug, 'So much for our profit.'

He had explained the financial situation to a non-financial audience in a manner that was easy to understand. Try to find new and simple methods of explaining complex material.

In this chapter I have not covered multi-media supported presentations as most business presenters usually do not have enough time for this. However, if you wish to incorporate video and sound, ensure your clips are no longer than 20 seconds. To get an insight into how multi-media can be used most successfully, watch TV news programmes. You will see how still images are interwoven with video, and how sound, including music and sound effects, can add emphasis.

I believe the Internet is also having a strong influence on design as well as providing a wealth of material for visual aids. Visit www.presentersonline.com for inspiration.

Hints on Using a Production Company

The range of services offered by production companies is vast and your choice will probably be dictated by your budget. You can use them to produce well-designed slides only, or you can hand over the entire organisation of your sales conference, including guest speakers and participants from around the world. This book doesn't aim to show you how to run a large-scale conference. However, I am including some suggestions here for using outside assistance that may help you to avoid some of the common pitfalls:

- *Key content* Appoint one person to be the principal point of contact within your organisation to work with the production company.

- *Advance planning* Contact the professionals as early as possible. If you are planning a large conference in a major city, contact them even before you have decided the date, as they may be able to help with your choice of venue.

- *Ask questions*   The professionals may talk in jargon and abbreviations but don't be put off by that. If you don't understand what they are talking about, ask.

- *Allow sufficient time*   You will naturally want to include the latest sales figures or the most recent data in your presentation, but don't make this an excuse for not providing the production company with scripts in plenty of time. If necessary, you can add the final figures later, but at least you can avoid the expense of having their staff working over weekends and evenings in order to prepare any last-minute visuals.

- *Late changes cost money*   Nothing is impossible, but everything costs money. Ensure that everyone, and that includes your chairperson, has prepared a script that won't need eleventh-hour changes. Remember that slides will be prepared to illustrate certain points in the script and if the words are changed, the visual may have to be scrapped.

SUMMARY

- Make sure you really need your visuals and that you're using them for the right reason.

- Make them simple, colourful, consistent and relevant.

- They should visually aid your talk and not distract from it with verbal printouts.

6

How to Look Professional When Using Visual Aids

'We are what we repeatedly do.
Excellence then is not an art but a habit'
ARISTOTLE

It is one thing to have excellent visuals to hand, but it's important to use them competently. Here are some tips to help you look professional.

Flip Charts

Always carry your own marker pens as they can dry out quickly and those supplied may not write well; also, you can be sure that you have the right thickness and colour for your purpose.

You can prepare the flip chart in advance, but if the paper is thin, only write on every other page, otherwise some of your audience will attempt to decipher what is written on the next page. Use block capitals in a variety of colours to ensure that your visual is easy to read and attractive to look at. Remember to hide your prepared flip chart until it is relevant so that it creates maximum impact. Flip chart pads are usually 60cm by

80cm, but they are also available in larger sizes and a smaller variety for use with desktop easels. If you are drawing graphs or working out calculations seek out paper printed with faint squares – they are invisible to the audience but make it easier to write in a straight line.

The height of some easels is adjustable. I remember seeing a short speaker struggling with a large piece of flip chart paper, trying to fold it over against a strong current from an air-conditioning duct. Practise turning the pages over and if there is any difficulty, lower the easel or arrange for one of your listeners to help you at the appropriate time.

Use a paper-clip or fold over the corner of the page to indicate your next visual or a visual to which you want to refer back during the course of your talk.

Flip charts are not suitable for large audiences so their use is limited to informal groups of approximately 25 people or fewer, and are used most effectively during the course of a presentation to note information given by members of the audience, to calculate, to show organisational change, to illustrate a management model or to highlight and summarise essential points. This can serve as a visual reminder and a listener who has been distracted can tune back in by glancing at the flip chart. Your main points on the flip chart can help you to summarise at the end of your talk. Consider using two flip charts so that one can display the key ideas, while the other is used as a scribbling pad.

I have seen a speaker at an internal meeting open her talk with a question to the audience: 'Now what do you think are the chief factors we need to consider about our new timetable?' As the audience responded she noted their points on the flip chart and addressed each in turn. Be sure you can anticipate what your listeners might say and you must also show why you are not accepting all of their answers; for example, 'I'm not going to write down Holiday Schedules because we will be discussing this in more detail at the meeting planned for Friday afternoon.' If you genuinely want a contribution from the listeners, it's important that your body language indicates this. Stand relaxed, but ready to write, making encouraging eye contact with each of them.

Using a flip chart in brain-storming sessions is helpful as it enables all the points to be visible to your group. As each sheet is completed you can tear it off and stick it on to the walls around the room so that you make up a complete picture.

Some speakers are reluctant to make use of the flip chart in front of the audience or during the course of their talk because they fear they won't be able to write clearly or, worst of all, their spelling will let them down. Use lined paper to overcome the first difficulty and bad spellers can always admit their weakness and ask for help from the audience. If you can anticipate some of the words you'll need to write, note them in pencil at the side of the flip chart; your audience won't be able to see them and you'll have a crib to refer to. If you are using the flip chart to summarise your main points, prepare it in pencil to be certain of the correct spacing of your letters and words. If you make a mistake while preparing your flip chart you can either tear off the sheet and start again or use white correcting fluid over the error, wait until it dries and write over it.

Writing clearly and quickly on the flip chart in front of an audience is not easy and, if you're planning to use it frequently, find time to practise as it's a skill that can be learnt.

Hints on using the flip chart

- Always remove the previous speaker's chart.

- Stand to one side of the easel, on the left if you're right-handed and on the right if you're left-handed, so that as you write you are not obstructing the audience's view; this position allows you to glance over your shoulder occasionally, to keep eye contact with your listeners. Also stand to one side of the easel if you are indicating points on the flip chart.

• Don't hang on to the easel for support.

• Never write and speak at the same time. This is one of the most difficult rules to follow but remember that anything that you say while you are writing will not be heard by your listeners; they will be concentrating on what you're writing and not listening, and your voice will be muffled as it will be directed at the flip chart and not at your audience.

• Don't hold a marker pen in your hand when you're not writing.

• Look at the audience and not at the flip chart. Speakers break this rule more often than any other because eye contact with the audience is difficult and looking at a familiar flip chart is comforting. Learn to overcome this problem and stand square to the audience and not half-turned to the flip chart.

The Overhead Projector

This visual aid is suitable for large and small audiences, and slides are easy to make. The smaller desk version can be carried to locations that don't have suitable equipment.

Use it as a scribbling pad

Most overhead projectors are used to project slides on to a screen, but when a roll of acetate film covers the top it can be used in a similar manner to a flip chart, i.e. to note down audience contributions, to summarise decisions, to show calculations or to use as a scribbling block for the speaker to illustrate theories and suppositions visually.

You can use pre-drawn diagrams or outlines and then complete them in front of the audience while explaining the significance of the additional material. Alternatively you can place an incomplete transparency under the acetate roll and draw on the finishing lines without marking a transparency you may want to use on another occasion.

As the speaker sits alongside the projector facing the audience, he can continue to make eye contact as he writes, which he can't do while using the flip chart. This secondary use of the overhead projector is generally more suited to lectures and informal training sessions.

Understanding the equipment

In order to get the most out of using the overhead projector, you should be familiar with each part of the equipment.

The screen

Try to match the screen size to the size of the audience and place it at least two screen widths from the front row and not more than five from the back row. Place it across a corner of the room rather than in the centre of a wall (see pages 214–15 for seating diagrams), and make sure the top of the screen can be tilted forward towards the projector to avoid the keystone effect (this is when the top of the projected slide is wider than the bottom – if it's not possible to adjust the screen, place something under the front of the projector to raise it). Bright lights and sunlight shining on the screen will mar the picture, so make arrangements to avoid this.

The projector

Very often projectors are placed on trolleys that fit them snugly but leave no space on which to put the transparencies. Try to find a low table with adequate room for the projector and the transparencies, and hopefully you will be able to project sufficiently high so that the top arm of the projector doesn't interfere with the audience's view. When the equipment is set up, sit in every seat to check that there is an unobstructed view of the screen. When the transparencies are being projected you may need to step to one side to avoid blocking the screen. If you are using the continuous roll of acetate as a scribbling block or to note down your summaries, remember to place a low chair next to the projector or you may end up squatting and attempting to write while not falling over. Get a colleague to check visibility when you are alongside the projector.

Transparencies

Place a transparency on the projector and aim to fill the screen, avoiding an uneven white border of light. You may have to move the projector backwards or forwards to adjust the picture size. Turn the knob on the vertical column to adjust the focus. If the projected image has brown corners, this is an indication that the bulb support should be raised or lowered. This can be achieved with the lamp brightness switch.

The bulb

Most projectors are designed to carry a spare bulb that is easily slipped into place by moving a small lever on the front of the projector.

Hints on using the OHP

• Always switch off the projector before removing your transparency. The speaker who waves her transparency over the projector is providing a minor distraction and a blank screen is unpleasant to look at. If you have a series of slides simply move the next slide into place without switching off.

• Point at the transparency and not at the screen. I have seen a speaker standing on tiptoe and apologise for not being able to reach the furthest corner of the screen to indicate some vital statistic, when all he had to do was to point at the transparency on the projector.

See also page 93 for some general hints on using projectors.

Laptop Computers

Laptop presentations have become very common and most managers are familiar with the basic elements of creating PowerPoint slides. However, some rely on their secretaries to produce slides, while others rely on their more technically minded colleagues to set up the equipment.

If you are in either of these categories, I recommend that you enrol on a PowerPoint training course as it will give you confidence that you will be able to cope if something goes wrong. A member of the audience may help you out, but your credibility and your self-esteem will have been dented. Spend time becoming familiar with the software programme and the equipment to run it.

The advantages of using laptop visuals are:

- new material can be incorporated e.g. up-to-the-minute accurate sales figures;

- presentations can be customised easily;

- the transitions between slides are smooth;

- text builds are hassle-free and key points can be highlighted;

- video clips can be added;

- colour, backgrounds and professional templates add impact.

The disadvantages are also all the points listed above. Presenters (and their audiences) can get carried away with the technology, so instead of adding value, the visuals hijack the presentation. (See also Chapter 5 How to Design Visual Aids.)

Equipment

Screen

If you are presenting to a couple of people you can do it directly from the laptop. Ensure that the screen is not catching any reflected light and that the image is visible to your listeners.

In the absence of a screen, or in a small space, you may wish to project directly on to a plain wall; however, you should expect a reduction in the quality of the image.

Where you position the screen will depend on how dominant you want your slides to be. If you are illustrating 80 per cent of your presentation, place the screen centrally; if only 20 per cent of your talk has visual support, *you* should be centre stage. Place the screen to your left which makes it easier for the audience to look from you to the screen and read visuals from left to right. See the layouts on pages 214–15.

For larger, more formal presentations you may wish to use

rear screen projection. The projector is placed behind the screen and is invisible to the audience. A special opaque screen is needed for back projection, together with a projector with a reverse image feature.

Projector

Data or LCD projectors are portable and usually used with a laptop. It is possible to download your presentation on to a memory card (PCMCIA) and eliminate the need for the laptop. However, some functions such as transitions will not be projected.

DLP (Digital Light Processing) projectors, particularly the three-chip design, give a better, clear picture, but you should aim for 750/800 ANSI lumens (which is the brightness measurement) for an audience of approximately 20. Some companies prefer to hire in projectors when they are needed as the technology is improving rapidly and a purchased projector can quickly be superseded by later models. Be sure to have an appropriate stand for the projector – an OHP trolley is too low.

Plasma screens are installed in some boardrooms and used as an alternative to a projector, and also double up as a monitor for video-conferencing. They are not portable so cannot replace the data projector for off-site presentations. Although the picture quality is very high, they can only be used for audiences of under fifteen because of their size.

Laptop

The rule of thumb for laptops is simple – get the fastest you can lay your hands on and always run it from the mains. I shall resist the temptation to recommend specifications because the IT world moves so rapidly that my suggestions will be almost instantly out of date.

Ensure you have a video display card if you want to show

clips and a video capture card so that you can input from TV, video or from your own camcorder. You will also need a sound card. Be aware of infringing copyright laws if you use audio or video that is not in the public domain. Video is very memory hungry and you will need a CD-ROM (and drive) and not a floppy disk for this type of presentation.

You could even fire up Netscape Navigator or Internet Explorer to show off your company's website. You would obviously need a phone line or a mobile phone if you wish to do this.

Hints on using a laptop with a data projector

• Always make a hard copy of your visuals, i.e. handouts and acetates in case of equipment failure.

• Put your presentation on *two* separate disks or CDs in case one of them has a fault.

• If possible put your presentation on the hard drive of your laptop to save time and hiccups with downloading the disk.

• Ensure that you have an extension lead if your presentation is away from your home base.

• Print out your visuals six to a page and number them as they appear in the slide sorter. This will enable you to locate a specific slide rapidly, perhaps in order to answer a question from the audience. This aide-mémoire will also help should you need to omit slides due to shortness of time. On your keyboard you simply press the number of the slide followed by Enter to project the slide.

• Allow double the time you think is sufficient to set up.

- Ensure that the laptop is connected to your projector and switch on the projector before you start up the computer.

- When you switch on your laptop you will notice that the presentation is only projected on the screen. In order to have them showing on both the screen and laptop, press Fn and F5 (on some laptops F4), and it will appear on the laptop only. Press Fn and F5 again and it will appear on both. This function is particularly useful if by accident you come out of your presentation or there is a technical hitch. You will be able to sort it out on the laptop without the audience seeing your frantic efforts.

- Switch off the screen saver on your laptop.

- The projected image should fill the screen and not overlap on to the wall or ceiling behind – use the zoom control on the projector for adjustment. If necessary, place a book under the projector if the legs are insufficient to raise it to an adequate height.

- Run through your presentation at least once with a data projector, as colour that works on the PC or laptop may change when projected.

- Experiment with the colour and contrast controls on the projector to get the best picture and, if necessary, switch off any overhead light in the room that shines directly on the screen.

- Check the volume of your speakers if the presentation contains an audio element.

- It is unnecessary to show a continuous stream of slides. Some areas of your presentation may require you to be the sole point of focus. Alternatively, you may be asked a question and wish to remove a slide while you answer. Press the B key on your keyboard and the screen will go black. Press it again and the image will reappear.

- Use a remote control if possible, so that you are not tied to the laptop when you want to advance slides.

- If you switch off the projector when it is not needed, for instance, over lunch, remember to allow one minute for it to warm up before you can project your next slide.

See also general hints on using a projector, below.

35mm Slides

It is important to remember that 35mm slides are not flexible. Once the carousel is loaded, it is impossible to change the order or omit slides during your talk. However, you can project 35mm slides more quickly and more smoothly than using an overhead projector.

They have the disadvantage of needing a darkened room, making it difficult for the audience to take notes or for the speaker to see the audience; you should arrange for a spotlight to shine on you during the slide show so that your listeners can see you and also to help you read your notes. Because of the need to change the lighting, your slides should not be sprinkled throughout your talk but shown together in one section.

If you are arranging a meeting or conference using 35mm slides, here is some of the equipment you will need.

The screen

Place the screen in the centre of the room and use a remote control to change slides. If this is not available you will need to work in close harmony with the projectionist to indicate the moment to move from one slide to another. For informal groups, you may choose to project the slides on to a suitable blank wall.

The projector

Place the projector directly in front of the screen, making sure that it doesn't obstruct the audience's view. The focus adjustment is generally located on the front of the projector around the lens, and you should ensure that there is a spare bulb and enough extension cable to reach the socket. Consider using two projectors to avoid the unprofessional blank screen at the point where the slide changes over. A twin dissolved unit adds an efficient touch to the presentation, and can be hired at a relatively low cost.

Slides

A carousel holds 80 slides, so try to avoid having 85 and have your slides mounted professionally in hinged cases with glass that can be easily cleaned. These ensure that the slide stays in focus, whereas the cheaper type tends to move in the projector.

The carousel

When you load your slides, stand by the carousel, looking towards the front of the room, following the beam of the projector's light, and hold the slide above the tray in a position so that you can read it. Place the slide in the carousel upside down, so that the top of the slide enters first. Many speakers make the mistake of turning the slide over before loading, which causes it to be projected back to front.

Hints on using 35mm slides

- Number all your slides and make sure your script is marked so that you know where each should appear.

- Double check that the carousel is correctly loaded.

- Practise your entire presentation at least twice, with the projectionist or by using remote control.

- Mark on the floor the exact position of the projector in case it is moved after the rehearsal.

- Use a pointer to indicate particular areas of interest, but put it down when not in use and resist the temptation to use it as a walking stick, or to conduct the audience like an orchestra.

General Hints on Using Projectors

Never switch on the projector without a visual in place. A blank, bright screen attracts everyone's eyes. If you doubt this, stand in front of a group and switch on the projector without a slide. You will see all eyes focused on the screen and, until you project a visual, everyone's mind will be in a state of anticipation for what is to come.

Allow enough time for your audience to absorb the content of your slide. I am often amazed that speakers who have obviously spent considerable time on producing excellent visuals leave them on view for such a short time. Remember, they may be very familiar to you, but the audience is seeing them for the first time and they require an adequate period to understand their full significance.

Prior to showing a complex visual, explain what it is intended to illustrate.

Allow a few moments of silence before commenting on the slide. The sense of sight is more powerful than the sense of hearing (one of the advantages of using visual aids), so your listeners will be looking and not listening.

Explain the visual when appropriate. This is not always necessary but it may speed up the audience's comprehension; certainly the main point of the visual should be repeated to help to reinforce it.

Never look at the screen yourself. Many professional speakers, who should know better, find the screen has a magnetism that forces them to keep looking at it. I have even seen speakers continue to look at the screen after they have switched off the projector. Your attention should be on the audience, even when they are looking at the screen. So, what happens if you suddenly get a blank mind and can't remember what is shining out behind you? Look at your laptop or overhead projector. Remember that no one will be persuaded by the back of your head – they need to see your face all the time.

Never walk between the projector and the screen. You will lose authority as your slide is projected on to your face and the light will dazzle you.

On an OHP use a pen, not your hand, to indicate. A hovering, possibly shaky finger over the transparency will be magnified on the screen, so place a pen or pencil (with a flat side to prevent it rolling off) on the projector to mark the relevant area. Use a pointer to indicate with a data or 35mm projector.

Remove the visual as soon as it is no longer relevant. If necessary use a logo slide when there is a section of your presentation that does not require visuals.

Use transitions with a laptop so that your information only appears when it is relevant. Fade down bullet points as you move on.

Never assume equipment will not be touched, moved or adjusted if you leave the room.

SUMMARY

- Familiarise yourself with the equipment.

- Rehearse *in situ*, including setting up and closing down.

- Have a back-up plan in case of equipment failure.

PART TWO

Presentation

7

Delivering Your Talk

'Speeches are like babies – easy to conceive and
difficult to deliver'
PAT O'MALLEY

Your talk has developed from ideas in your head to words on
the page, but until you have conveyed these thoughts to the
audience you will not have achieved your objective. In this
chapter I am going to describe four methods of delivery that
you can use and I will explain the advantages and disadvantages
of each of them.

Reading a Paper

Reading from a paper is the worst method that you can choose
and you should try and avoid it. It is particularly ineffective for
small groups, but there are many disadvantages whatever the
size of the audience.

An impressive speaker has sincerity, enthusiasm and vitality,
and unless you are a professional actor you will find it difficult
to express these emotions when you are reading.

Consider some of the other disadvantages:

- You can't keep good eye contact – one of the essential elements of effective speaking.

- Your body language is restricted – your script is like a ball and chain limiting your movements.

- You will sound unnatural and therefore insincere.

- Script dependence will mean you will never learn to be a convincing speaker or develop self-confidence.

There may be some occasions when you can't avoid reading a script, so Chapter 15 Writing and Reading Scripts for Conferences includes advice on writing spoken English and techniques to improve your reading aloud skills.

Memorising Your Script

Memorising your script is another method to be avoided because all your energy will be directed inwards instead of outwards to your audience. They will feel an invisible barrier and a lack of warmth, even if they don't understand the reason for it. Your talk will sound mechanical and will lack the vital ingredients of *enthusiasm* and *spontaneity*.

I remember seeing a speaker, who had a very eloquent and impressive style, with well-balanced sentences and a wide vocabulary, suddenly start to stumble halfway through his speech. He referred to his notes but never regained his confidence. It transpired that he had a photographic memory and had attempted to memorise the entire speech, but when his memory had let him down, he couldn't find his place in the script. In a second he lost credibility as he changed from being a fluent and articulate speaker to being hesitant and uncertain.

Although you may think you know your talk word for word, nerves can have an adverse effect on your memory and, unless you are very quick-thinking, you could find yourself floundering. By all means memorise certain passages that you are anxious to include, but don't rely on your memory for the entire speech.

So, if you shouldn't read a speech and you shouldn't memorise it and you can't make up an entire talk off the top of your head, how can you put across your message?

Speaking Extemporaneously (or Planned Improvisation)

This is the most effective delivery style as it has all the benefits of impromptu speaking and none of the drawbacks of reading. Your talk is prepared carefully, with a punchy beginning, a logical structure and a conclusive ending; it's well rehearsed and you can use brief outline notes to give you the confidence to sound enthusiastic, behave with vitality and look at the audience with sincerity.

What happens if I get a blank mind?

All speakers who speak extemporaneously have a safety net and you must decide which type is most appropriate for you and your talk.

There are several possibilities. However, if you have dipped into this chapter without having read Part One, you may want to look at it now, as you will find it easier to understand what follows.

Using your mind map as a safety net

You will recall that on the mind map you put all possible facts and details about the subject of your talk and you didn't attempt to evaluate them or fit them into a structure. At the next stage you studied the map to choose the ideas most appropriate for helping you achieve your objective in regard to your particular audience.

If you are using the mind map as your safety net you'll find the original map contained many fruitful ideas that were later discarded, so you will need to draw a second map that shows only the essential arguments and material. Draw the ideas in a logical sequence following a clockwise direction so that when you are delivering your talk you can simply glance occasionally at the map to reassure yourself that you are including all the salient points.

A mind map has the advantage of being visual and displays your talk in its entirety. This is helpful if you need to cut or condense during the course of your presentation. The details of your talk should be well known to you, so you will only need a prompt of a few words if your memory fails you. Sometimes your mind may go blank between ideas; you finish one point and suddenly realise you can't remember what comes next. You only need a nudge or a few words to set you off again. Often it's the structure or the sequence of points you forget, not the ideas themselves. The mind map can put you back on track when this happens.

You may feel that a mind map could be ambiguous or confusing – supposing you lost your place and couldn't remember which path you were on? If you are unsure of the benefit of the mind map as a safety net consider some of these other prompts you can use when speaking without a script.

Your script as a safety net

In your preparation, you will have moved through the following stages:

- researching the audience;

- setting an objective;

- drawing a mind map;

- choosing a path.

I have suggested in Chapter 3 How to Construct a Presentation that you may not need to write out a full script, but simply note key ideas on cards; if you don't work with a script, you can't use it as a prompt. However, if you do have a written script this doesn't mean reading every word.

Use a coloured pen to underline the key ideas so that they are conspicuous. As you rehearse, you should aim to describe each idea and link it with the next one without reading or memorising the words in your script. Simply glance at it from time to time to check the next point. If you employ alternative phrases and words during your practice, your talk will be fresh and different every time you rehearse. Using a script in this way increases your ability to speak fluently and decreases your dependence on the prepared text.

The key ideas are highlighted to assist you to follow your predetermined structure but you have the freedom to use your own choice of words to travel from one point to the next. Practise speaking round each point and don't be tempted to rely on the script; you should only use it as a guide to your destination and not as a vehicle to take you there.

Using confidence cards as a safety net

This is my own preferred prompt, as I find the mind map can sometimes be misleading and the script safety net can be too detailed; confidence cards combine the advantages of both without the drawbacks of either.

You can prepare confidence cards directly from your mind map, or from your full script. Remember that confidence cards should never contain full sentences as you don't read the cards – you only glance at them in moments of uncertainty. Eloquent phrases and clever ideas will only confuse you. Sometimes clients tell me that because of their nerves they can't see what is written on their cards, but frequently I find that their cards are closely covered with fully written sentences. These are not a help – they are a hindrance.

How to write confidence cards

Look at your script or mind map and mark the key points in red; next check the links you have used to move from one point to another and mark these in blue. If you have included anecdotes and illustrations, mark these in green. This will provide the skeleton of your talk.

Using 102mm by 152mm index cards write out in capital letters your key points, your links and your illustrations in the order in which they appear in your talk. Write on one side of the cards only.

If you are working from a full script, you must be very self-disciplined to avoid including all your persuasive phrases and scintillating sentences. Only single key words will help you.

Remember it's *your* speech with *your* ideas so you don't have to absorb and learn a host of alien concepts that you might forget. You only need learn the sequence of ideas and the links between them to give a good talk.

I restrain myself from writing too much on my cards by considering whether I would be able to continue my talk without a particular word or phrase. Often I find that I reject it because it's not central to my talk. I have included it because it was a particularly clever turn of phrase.

The test for the effectiveness of your confidence cards is how few words you have on them, not how many.

Why cards?

I suggest you use 102mm by 152mm cards, because they are less distracting than paper. You can hold them in your hand, or rest them on the lectern or table and you will look professional. Should you suffer from trembling hands, cards won't reveal this as much as a flapping piece of paper.

What's on them?

As well as reducing your talk to key words and ideas, on your confidence cards you can add instructions to yourself such as 'smile', 'look at the audience', 'stand still', etc., and you can mark the point where you want to use a visual aid or write on the flip chart.

Only two full sentences

Although it's essential to mark only key words on your cards, there are two exceptions to this rule. To give a strong framework you can write out in full the opening and closing sentences of your talk. You will probably find that your anxiety is at its highest point immediately before you speak and it's reassuring to see in front of you the exact words with which you'll begin. Similarly, you will need a clear end to your talk and if the final sentence is written out in full, you will be able to resist the temptation to run past the finishing post.

Memorising the opening and closing sentences can also be a boost to your confidence and will enable you to make positive eye contact with your listeners at the two periods in your talk when you know you are likely to have their maximum attention.

You should also write out in full any quotations you intend to include as it's essential to use the exact words.

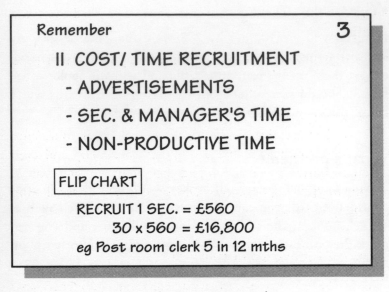

Speaker's prompt card

Remember to number them

Although some speakers tie a treasury tag through a punched hole to keep the cards together, I prefer to keep them untied as this allows me to take out cards or add to them. If they are untied, be sure to number them, because dropping unnumbered cards moments before you speak would be a calamity.

What are the advantages?

Using confidence cards will help you to:

- Sound natural – because you will be choosing your own words as you speak;

- Be confident – because you will have a safety net in the event of a blank mind;

- Look at the audience – because you won't need to read a script;

- Use expressive body language – because you will be free to move.

Show *sincerity*, *enthusiasm* and *vitality*.

If you have to give the same talk several times confidence cards will allow you to use a different vocabulary and even different illustrations for each audience. This will help you to remain fresh and spontaneous and prevent the material from becoming repetitious for you.

Suppose I leave something out?

Clients who have not had experience of using confidence cards tell me they are concerned that they may leave something out. Sometimes a participant on a course will resume his place, having given his presentation and as the other participants are congratulating him he shakes his head saying 'No, no, it wasn't any good, I forgot to say . . .'

My response is 'So what?' If you omit a passage, no one is aware of it but you. It will probably be a tiny percentage of the whole and although you would have liked to include it, rarely will such an omission affect the total impact of your talk. Don't dwell on what you have forgotten – instead, accept the praise for what you have remembered.

One word of warning – if you discover that you have omitted a passage while you are still speaking, beware of trying to backtrack in order to include it. You may confuse the audience. Should you feel that it is essential and cannot be omitted, don't apologise for leaving it out. Simply refer to it as an additional point that your listeners may want to consider, and remember to put it into context so that the audience can follow your structure. Often listeners know that their concentration is poor and even if you announce that you have four points to make and fail to include one of them, the audience will believe that the error is theirs and that they have misheard you.

If you have never used notes before and have always depended upon a full script, I urge you, during your practice sessions, to dispense with your script and try a few dry runs using only your cards. You will feel a great sense of freedom after your second or third attempt. If you are not prepared to risk dispensing with your script, try reducing some of it to key words and bullet points. This will enable you to look at the audience and talk spontaneously from time to time.

Pitfalls to avoid with confidence cards

Using confidence cards effectively will allow you to be an enthusiastic and sincere speaker but beware of these pitfalls:

• Don't shuffle or play with them during your talk.

• Don't keep staring at them to avoid looking at the audience.

• Don't use fillers, e.g. 'eh, umm, you know, I mean' etc., as you choose your words – remember the power of the silent pause.

Visual aids as a safety net

Provided you plan to stand or sit close to the projector, you can write prompts to yourself on the notes pages of your PowerPoint presentation. A few key words should be sufficient to provide a structure that you can follow easily.

Visual aids themselves can also act as a prompt but beware of using unimaginative and wordy slides simply to provide cues for yourself during your talk. In Chapter 5 How to Design Visual Aids, I recommended that they should contain a minimum of words to be effective. Using words on the visual aid merely as a prompt is a misuse of it and an insult to the audience. During a talk, words are for speaking not for reading.

I sometimes use a visual during a training session on body language. I draw a stick man on the flip chart and as I emphasise the importance of eye contact, and using hand gestures, I indicate these parts on the drawing. This helps to reinforce my message and also acts as a visual prompt for me.

Using a combination of creative visuals and confidence cards provides you with an effective safety net which won't prevent you from looking at your audience and using appropriate gestures.

Impromptu Speaking

'Impromptu speeches aren't worth the paper
they're written on'
LORD GODDARD

One of Winston Churchill's critics said, 'Winston has spent the best years of his life preparing his impromptu speeches.' It was actually a compliment; clever speakers are always prepared.

In fact you can often anticipate when you might be expected to 'say a few words'. Prior to a business meeting, study the agenda as it might suggest the topics on which you could be asked to comment. Informal meetings or leaving parties may not schedule a speaker, but you could anticipate whether you would be the best person to make a toast or offer a few words of praise.

Good impromptu speeches are prepared with as much care as any others and delivered so skilfully that they appear effortless. A true impromptu speech arises with no preparation time, so, if the situation might occur, plan how you would respond. Remember that every day of your life you are speaking without preparation so you know you have the ability to do so. Don't allow self-consciousness to hamper your self-expression. Some speakers collect short quotes or anecdotes they can deliver on the spur of the moment and which are appropriate for semi-formal occasions.

If you are asked to speak unexpectedly in a business meeting you can use one or two of the following techniques:

- Pause thoughtfully, admit you have not prepared, but don't apologise.

- Pick a structure, e.g. past, present, future; problem/solution.

- Build on the earlier speaker's comments or summarise what has been said previously. This is probably the easiest way to start.

- Restate the problem and add your own views.

- Agree with the other speakers – and decline to comment further.

- Use mental prompts such as Why? How? Which? When? What? Who? to build up your talk.

- Tell an anecdote – this is particularly effective if it is personal or humorous.

- Switch topics – 'Quality control is obviously important, but maybe we should be looking at it from another viewpoint. How can we hold on to our staff once they are trained?'

- End with a quote, e.g. 'I know that you believe you have understood what you think I said, but I am not sure you realise that what you heard is not what I meant.'

SUMMARY

- Speak extemporaneously.

- Choose a suitable safety net.

- Practise several times aloud, preferably with a tape recorder or on video.

8

Techniques for Handling Nerves

'There are only two types of speakers: those who get
nervous and liars'
MARK TWAIN

'Before they get up, they do not know what they are going
to say; when they are speaking, they do not know what
they are saying; and when they have sat down, they do
not know what they have said'
CHURCHILL (on Lord Charles Beresford, 1912)

Everyone Suffers From Nerves

Once you have decided the best way to deliver your talk the
next thing to consider is how to handle those inevitable nerves.
You may find it difficult to believe, but even the most accomplished performers suffer from nerves. Paddy Ashdown, leader
of the Liberal Democratic Party for many years, said that he
viewed Question Time in the House of Commons 'with
terror'. This from a man who in his younger years was a tough
SAS soldier.

Actor Daniel Day Lewis left the stage during a performance

at the National Theatre because of nerves. Actor and comedian Stephen Fry actually left the country because of the pressures of performing in front of audiences.

When a speaker fails to feel nervous, the chances are that the speaker has become complacent and boring. You need nerves to give you sparkle, but what you don't want are nerves that cripple you and prevent you from performing well. So, in this book, I won't show you how to kill the butterflies but I will show how you can train them to fly in formation.

First Catch Your Butterflies

In this chapter I will look at what makes you nervous, how it feels and how you can overcome it.

Immediately I see that I have set myself an impossible task. How can I know what makes *you* nervous and how it feels for *you?* So, you're going to have to help me. You will need some paper and a pen to get the most out of this chapter. Pause for a moment in your reading and make a list of all the physical and mental manifestations of nerves you have when you speak to a group of people. This is your list. If you have trouble remembering, think of the last time you were embarrassed – *where* did it affect you? In your face? Your stomach? Your hands?

You might find that just thinking about feeling nervous produces some of the symptoms. If so, observe them and try to measure your level of anxiety on a scale of one to ten. One is the lowest level of anxiety and ten is the highest level. Speaking in public is never a ten because if you were trapped in a locked car on a level crossing with a train bearing down on you facing instant death you would probably be feeling worse. Speaking in public might feel like death but you wouldn't die; it won't kill you. In a survey in the US, 3,000 people were asked to list their ten worst fears and speaking in public came out as number one ahead of death, financial ruin, spiders and snakes.

You may sympathise with this view but do remember that death is permanent and speaking in public is not.

What Colour is Fear?

Do you think of a colour when you think of fear? No? So try and describe in words what your nervousness actually looks like: what colour is it, what shape does it have, does it move? Take it out of your body and look at it. Keep it there for a moment while I list some of the symptoms that my clients have come up with over the years:

- shaking knees, palpitating heart and churning stomach;
- tight throat and unable to swallow, dry mouth or too much saliva;
- wet palms, feeling very hot, blushing and feeling cold;
- blank mind, unable to focus on audience or notes and feeling faint;
- stuttering, shortness of breath, nervous laugh and trembling voice.

You may recognise many of these and you might even suffer from some symptoms that aren't on the list. I find that I sweat a lot when I am nervous, but fortunately only under my arms and not on my face so that it doesn't show. I also find that my heart beats extra fast and that my stomach churns.

The colour of my fear and nervousness is black and dark green and looms about me in a threatening cloud and I think it's laughing at me, but you know a strange thing happens when I actually have the courage to look at it. It seems to become smaller. Try to examine your nervousness without allowing it to threaten you. Just acknowledge its presence without any dread. Just think about the feeling and try to put it outside yourself. I know it's not easy, but the more you try, the less frightening it will become.

What Makes You Nervous?

I can't answer that question for you, so again you will have to make a list for yourself of all the disasters that could happen to you. *List as many fears as you can.* Remember it's the fears that are making you nervous. Imagine you are in your next speaking situation and you are feeling terrified, or imagine you have been asked to speak, or even that you are in a meeting and want to speak but something is holding you back. What is it?

Is it fear of any of these things happening?

- Forgetting what you want to say. Not making sense. Being boring.

- People disagreeing, asking difficult questions, even getting up and walking out.

- Your boss thinking that you are an idiot.

- Letting down your subordinates, colleagues and friends.

- Being judged and found wanting – by yourself or others.

You may see from your own list that some of your fears are not unique. It's quite reassuring on my courses to find that many fears are shared; even the person who appears to be most confident worries about looking foolish. Everyone has an insecure centre. The next time you see a good speaker, ask her how she felt beforehand and, if she is prepared to be honest, I am sure you will find that she, too, suffers from nerves.

The great truth

Now we have discovered the great truth of public speaking –
everyone suffers from nerves and everyone is frightened of
looking foolish. Think about that for a minute because it's very
reassuring. You are not any different from anyone else. You
may be thinking that if other people felt as nervous as you, they
could not speak as well as they do. You may be thinking that
your nerves are worse than anyone else's. They are not. The
nerves are the same, the difference is that you have not learnt
to control your nerves – they are controlling you.

Negative thoughts or positive power?

Do you dislike feeling nervous? You may think it's absurd to
ask such a question, but try to learn to welcome your anxiety
because you need it to be a good speaker. It is the force that
drives your motor and without it you will be dull and uninspiring; you need to harness its power to give you positive
energy or it will dominate you and cause crippling panic.
Regard it as part of the equation in the same way you regard
other feelings. Before taking off your jacket you feel hot; before
eating you feel hungry; before going to bed you feel tired; and
before speaking in public you feel nervous.

What are you really afraid of?

Earlier I asked you to look at the shape and colour of your
nerves. This may have been difficult, but now I'm going to
show you how to get to know and understand your nervousness, so that you can take the first steps towards gaining control
and turning negative nerves into positive power. But I can only
do this if you are willing to co-operate in a painful exercise. If
you are reading this in a bookshop, I suggest you go to the cash

desk immediately, because you will need a quiet half-hour by yourself if the next section is to have any lasting effect on you. Take the book home and only open it again when you know you can concentrate on it.

How to Control Your Nerves

Imagine that you are at your next speaking function, you are about to begin speaking, you look around and you see people waiting for you to start. How does it feel? What is your level of anxiety? And as you stand there, what are your fears? *What is your worst fear*? Can you identify it? What is the most awful thing that could happen to you as you stand there? Think about it in detail because it's about to happen. Don't close your mind to it, just let it happen and feel the total horror and your inability to control the situation. It is getting worse and you can do nothing. Dwell for a few moments on the feelings that you are experiencing as you imagine your greatest fear.

After a time you do manage to get out of the more public arena and you find that you are shaking all over. Never, never again you say to yourself, never again will they get me to speak in front of an audience. You feel humiliated, mortified and ashamed. Examine the horror and dwell on it – remember this is only in your imagination so you can escape from it at any stage, but it might be best if you stayed with it for a few moments more. Imagine how you would feel, what you would say, what you would do, how you would live through that terrifying experience. Put down this book so you can concentrate on your worst fear. If you can force yourself to face up to your worst possible fear, you will be going a long way towards controlling your nerves.

On one of my courses I had a manager who feared the audience walking out – he gave presentations to audiences of 150 people – and imagined that as he was speaking first one person and then another and then small groups began standing up and making for the exit. He was left with five or six people scattered about a large hall. He imagined the whole scene, how he eventually left the stage, and how he felt afterwards.

A young woman trainer confided to me that she was always fearful that the accountants whom she taught might challenge her right to be training: 'What real qualifications do you have?' As she was self-taught she felt particularly vulnerable. She imagined the training room and the senior partner who challenged her. She imagined her bumbling answer. She imagined the terrifying scene as the rest of the group lost confidence in her and how she felt during the lecture and afterwards.

Let's go back to your most terrifying moment and imagine that already 24 hours have passed; but you have not discussed your disaster with anyone because it's still too painful. You feel you can confide in a close friend maybe and you relive the whole situation. It still feels terrible, but remember you lived through it – *you did not die.*

Now look forward a month and imagine you are telling a group of friends about the experience and you find that one or two of them have had similar experiences and are very sympathetic. You are beginning to see this experience as an event in the past. Try looking forward a year, and in a pub or at a party you meet someone who was at the scene of your humiliation; he comes over and speaks to you and reminds you that he was present: 'Glad I wasn't in your shoes, if only you could have seen the look on your face – it was a scream.' You find that now a year has passed you can smile and chuckle at the memory.

You may have read quickly to the end of this section to see what the outcome was going to be. I would urge you to try this exercise and examine your worst fears and feelings. Some people have told me that their job is on the line if they don't perform well at a major presentation, others have told me that their reputation as an expert in their field might be jeopardised, or that a major contract worth millions of pounds might be lost if the speaker fails to be persuasive. Whatever your own personal fear is, remember that it can't kill you. You will live beyond it and you may even be able to smile at the situation in the future. Remember that for this exercise to work, you must not stop at the moment of the disaster, but continue through to the following 24 hours, the following month and the following year.

How Could You Have Coped Better?

Now that you have faced your worst fear and lived through it, try looking back at how you could have prevented it or coped better if it were to happen again. You will be tempted to ignore it, but if you can have the self-discipline to confront it, you will find that you can learn from the situation. You will gain confidence by aiming at a positive outcome.

Try reliving your worst fear again. It may be too difficult to do immediately, so read another chapter and come back to it later. On your second attempt, you can imagine yourself coping successfully with a difficult situation. Once again, imagine it in full detail; how you felt, what you said and how other people reacted. Only allow yourself to imagine a positive outcome. You may need to pause in order to choose your behaviour or find the right words; do so. This is your fantasy, so you are in charge. Of course you may also realise that your fears are ridiculous and completely groundless – that can be very reassuring.

For instance, my young female accountancy trainer, when challenged by a senior partner in her scenario, imagined how she would smile and walk towards him. She would say, 'My qualifications are not on paper but they are very real. They are the hundreds of men and women who have been promoted in this firm due to my training.' This exercise helped her to cope with her worst fear.

I hope that exercise has helped you to see that there is life after failure. You have faced your worst fear, coped with it and lived through it, so you can now concentrate on being a success. Now you are ready to turn nerves into a positive force.

Converting Panic into Positive Power

In this section, I am going to suggest a number of techniques you can use to harness your nervous energy.

- Practice is your best defence against failure. Follow the suggestions in Chapter 14 Practising and Rehearsing, and practise aloud several times in front of a long mirror so that you can become familiar with every point of your talk. Remember to continue to the end in every practice session, because you don't want to have an over-rehearsed first half and a poor, stuttering second half. Find out as much as you can about the venue, seating arrangements, lighting and equipment, so that you feel comfortable with it.

- Try to visualise your success – create a picture for yourself of the scene immediately after you've spoken. Imagine your clients looking pleased and stimulated by your presentation, or your sales force feeling motivated to work harder, or your board of directors nodding in agreement, or a large audience clapping enthusiastically. Whoever your audience is, think of them reacting in a very positive manner. Try to paint a vivid picture of the situation, including your own feelings of relief and pleasure. Don't allow any negative thoughts to intrude – this is your success. The more you concentrate on this, the greater your chance of it becoming true.

- You could imagine you are an actor playing the part of a successful and confident speaker.

- Remember a good feeling – think back to a particular personal success, e.g. the day you were given a rise, when you were praised by the chairman, when you achieved the highest sales. Recall a day of personal achievement when you were proud of yourself and it felt good to be alive. This is your own kitty of confidence and you can tap into it whenever you feel a moment of doubt. You have achieved in the past and you can achieve in the future.

• Examine the positive aspects of nerves – ask yourself 'What is the benefit of feeling nervous?' You may be surprised to recognise that there is actually an advantage in having butterflies.

Coping with the Physical Symptoms

If you know you sweat, wear a lightweight outfit and carry a handkerchief to dab your face and your hands if necessary.

If you suffer from a dry mouth limit the amount of water you drink. Instead place your tongue across your teeth and gently bite it – your saliva will begin to run. Another trick is to put the tip of your tongue at the top of your mouth and say a silent LLL sound which will also help you to overcome a dry mouth.

Trembling hands will only be noticeable if you hold sheets of paper, so use cards.

If your throat tightens up and your voice becomes restricted before you face the audience, try yawning to relax it. Lift your lips away from your teeth like an animal snarling, open your mouth as wide as possible so that the muscles on your neck stick out and you hear a roaring in your ears. Now the yawn should start to take over and it will relax your whole face, neck and throat. You can't feel tense while yawning as it is a great relaxer, like laughing.

If you suffer from breathlessness, take deep breaths. Shallow breaths mean that you sound odd and you feel panicky. We take in breaths automatically, but we have to think about letting the air out, so remember to breathe in to the count of two and exhale slowly to the count of four.

I hope that some of these suggestions will work for you but bear in mind that you are not aiming to kill the butterflies – only to control them. You need their power to be an effective speaker; so use them, don't be frightened of them and regard them as old friends.

SUMMARY

- Everyone suffers from nerves.

- Don't let your nerves control you.

- Face up to your fears.

- Turn negative nerves into positive power.

- Practice kills panic.

- You *will* be successful.

9

Relaxation Exercises

'The brain is a wonderful organ. It works perfectly until the moment you stand up to speak in public'

ANON

In this chapter I am going to describe some techniques for relaxing, which you can practise at any time you are feeling tense, as well as in the final moment before you begin to speak.

Why is Relaxing Important?

If you can relax the tension in your muscles, you'll find that your voice will sound more sincere, your gestures will look natural and you will use fewer non-words and fillers. As you learn to control your nerves and feel more confident, your muscles will relax automatically. Here are some exercises to help you in the process.

Getting into the Habit

I once attended a seminar on hypnotism and was selected by the hypnotist as a guinea pig. He taught me how to self-hypnotise so that when I found myself in a minor panic about being late for an appointment, I could park the car and sit for 60 seconds, and allow myself to go into a mild trance. Then I would arrive in a more relaxed frame of mind. Unfortunately, I failed to keep practising this technique and I'm not able to use it any more, but I have retained the memory of how my body feels when it's untensed. Some people don't have that awareness. 'What do you mean relaxed – I am relaxed!' they say through clenched teeth.

EXERCISE 1   Feel the tension

In order to learn how to relax, you must first feel the tension. Start with your toes and curl them up as tight as possible, hold this position for 30 seconds and then release. Next, tense your calf muscles, hold for 30 seconds and release; tense your thigh muscles and buttocks, hold for 30 seconds and release; then tense your stomach and chest, hold for 30 seconds and release; tense your shoulders and neck, hold for 30 seconds and release; and finally, tense your face, hold and release. There is no need to rush this exercise – do it slowly to get the maximum benefit.

You can practise this exercise before you fall asleep at night and you'll notice a warm, tingly feeling all over your body. By being aware of the contrast between your tensed and relaxed muscles, you'll get into the habit of being able to relax at will. You'll simply recognise your tension and tell your body to let go. It's impossible to be relaxed and anxious at the same time. This exercise will only work for you in moments of high stress (like speaking to an audience) if you have practised it sufficiently in unstressed moments.

Learning to be Centred

This is fundamental to performing. An uncentred performer on the stage looks like an amateur and an uncentred speaker inevitably feels tense. Your centre, your 'point of power', is situated roughly at the solar plexus, above the navel.

EXERCISE 1   **Becoming centred**

To help you to be centred stand straight, bend your knees slightly, close your eyes and concentrate on your feet. Feel each toe digging into the floor as though you were curling your toes in sand. Now squat, keeping your feet flat on the floor. Imagine that your legs are pillars of iron connected to the centre of the earth. Rest your hands on your knees for balance. Stay there until you can feel your centre of gravity lowering to your pelvis. Rise slowly, straighten up and breathe.

EXERCISE 2   **Centring and posture**

This exercise also helps with your posture: stand sideways before a full-length mirror and bend your knees slightly. Notice how your pelvis and buttocks are out of alignment with your back. Now place your hands on your hips and gently roll your pelvis forward, pulling your stomach in and down. Your buttocks should now be aligned directly under your back in a straight line. Now imagine a string running all the way up your spine and out of the top of your head. Let the string hold you like a puppet. This exercise centres you and enables you to use natural and graceful movements.

Five Minutes to go and in Private

EXERCISE 1 **Be a rag doll**

Allow your body to flop down from the waist and swing your arms like a rag doll. If no one can hear you, say 'I don't care – I don't care – I don't care' as you hang loosely. This will get rid of the tension in your upper body.

EXERCISE 2 **Shoulders on parade**

Pull your shoulders right up to your ears and let go; repeat this exercise five times to release the tension in your neck and shoulders. Roll your shoulders backwards four times and roll them forwards four times. Roll your head over your right shoulder, let it hang backwards, then bring it round over your left shoulder and finally rest your chin on your chest. Reverse the direction and repeat four times. This exercise helps to relax throat and neck muscles.

EXERCISE 3 **Wibbly wobbly**

Shake your hand from your wrist and then your arm from your shoulder and finally let all your upper body shake, including your head and lips.

EXERCISE 4 **Horse laugh**

Loosen your lips and blow through them like a horse.

EXERCISE 5 **Facial exercises**

Stretch your lips into a silent E and purse them into a silent O and now rapidly say a silent E, O, E, O. Repeat ten times. This is an excellent exercise to release those muscles around the mouth that can make you look severe when you are feeling nervous.

EXERCISE 6 **Yawn**

On page 120 I have described how to make yourself yawn at will by opening your mouth as wide as you can. This will relax your neck, throat and mouth area.

One Minute to go and in Public

Tense all your muscles (not your face this time) and release. Repeat twice. Breathe deeply and exhale fully. Concentrate on your rhythmic, slow, deep breathing. Be curious about your surroundings and your audience. See how many red ties you can count. If you are in a small group, look at everyone's suit and note the different patterns in the fabrics.

Think of a peaceful scene – walking through a pine forest, lying on a warm beach, the view from a hill across several green fields on an autumn afternoon – feel a deep inner stillness and quiet confidence.

Think positive thoughts and you will be a success.

Exercises to Aid Relaxation

EXERCISE 1 **Breathing**

Under stress breathing becomes short and shallow. By controlling your breathing pattern you can have a direct effect on your anxiety. Sit back and close your eyes. Relax your shoulders and concentrate on your breathing. Place one hand on your stomach. As you breathe in feel your stomach moving out. Slowly breathe out and feel it moving in like a deflating balloon. With each breath hold it a second longer before you *slowly* breathe out. Repeat ten times for maximum benefit.

EXERCISE 2   **Shoulder raises/rolls**

Bring your shoulders up to your ears – hold up to touch your ears – hold and release. Repeat five times. Slowly roll your shoulders forward for a repeat of five and then roll backwards.

EXERCISE 3   **Facial exercises**

Push all your features to the tip of your nose five times. Push your features to the back of your head five times.

EXERCISE 4   **Shake off your nerves**

Shake your hands and arms as if you're trying to get rid of something sticking to your fingers – this will get your blood flowing. Repeat with each leg.

EXERCISE 5   **Relax your throat**

Slowly yawn. If this is difficult, open your mouth as wide as you can and keep it open – a yawn will appear from nowhere.

EXERCISE 6   **Relax your lips**

Blow through your lips to make a sound like an outboard engine on a boat. This will prevent your upper lip sticking to your teeth when you begin to talk.

EXERCISE 7   **Mind games**

To calm your mind walk from one side of the room to the other counting backwards from twenty to one.

SUMMARY

- Learn some simple relaxation techniques.

- The more your practise loosening up when you feel tense, the more automatically your body will relax.

- As you grow more at ease with giving a presentation you will appear more assured, thus creating a positive cycle of relaxation and confidence.

10

How to Look Confident

'Great dancers are not great because of their technique;
they are great because of their passion'
MARTHA GRAHAM, dancer and choreographer

Once you have controlled your butterflies you need to concentrate on looking confident. You will never make a successful speaker if you only have a good speech; in fact you could even be an effective speaker without a good speech. Some speakers can spend so long searching for the exact word, the imaginative example or the eloquent turn of phrase that they lose sight of those vital qualities that will ensure their success in front of an audience.

We have seen that audiences are not impressed with words. They are impressed with:

- enthusiasm;

- vitality;

- sincerity.

The Day of Judgement

Even before you open your mouth, your audience will have made several assumptions about you and, in the light of their own experience and prejudices, you will have scored plus or minus points. If you think this is unfair, consider your own internal conversation as you sit in on a train or watch pedestrians from your traffic-jammed car – aren't you assessing and judging the people you see? We all do it to everyone we come in contact with, and audiences as a whole are no different; they are curious about the speaker who will be part of their lives for the duration of the talk. You never have a second opportunity to make a first impression, so whether you are entering a room for an interview, an informal meeting or an annual conference, your audiences will assess you from the moment they can see you.

Look Happy!

Human beings have a very simple way of showing friendship, and yet judging by how little it is used, you would think it was very difficult and extremely expensive. Smiling at your audience says, 'I am happy to be here and I am glad you are here too.' I expect that you will be feeling the exact opposite, but that is the very reason why you should smile.

Why let everyone know you are feeling nervous? No one can see your pounding heart or churning stomach or your dry mouth, so why reveal on your face the turmoil that's going on inside your body? If you think that smiling is inappropriate for your position or your subject, reconsider your view because I am sure your audience would like to welcome a friendly rather than an unfriendly speaker. Even an undertaker smiles in sympathy. Remember you don't need an ear-to-ear grin, only an 'I am happy to be here and glad you are here too' expression.

How to Make an Entrance

You have fixed your 'I am happy' expression on your face. You enter the interview room, lecture hall or meeting venue and you walk confidently to a chair or podium. You are making a first impression so let your body language say, 'Here is a worthwhile and interesting person.' In a small group, you will probably be shaking hands, always remembering to maintain eye contact and murmuring pleasantries about the weather, the cricket score or your/their journey, as you sit down. If you are speaking at a large conference centre, you will know what to expect because you will have rehearsed your entrance already. (See Chapter 15 Writing and Reading Scripts for Conferences.)

Once settled, you can look around and take a few quiet, deep breaths. Don't look at your notes or even touch them. No amount of silent rehearsing will help you make a better speech at this stage. Instead concentrate on what is happening about you and listen to the other speakers. For many people these final few moments before they speak are the worst, but try not to let yourself be controlled by feelings of panic – you should be well rehearsed and looking forward to giving a good performance.

Why is Body Language Important?

However you look or move, you will be giving off signs to your audience as to your inner feelings – you cannot not communicate. Being aware of your particular mannerisms and nervous gestures enables you to correct them and present a confident unselfconscious image.

In spite of my experience, I am always apprehensive standing in front of an audience, but people tell me that I look totally in control and relaxed. In fact I am in control, but I am *not* relaxed; that might sound uncomfortable to you as maybe you are aiming to be a casual, informal and unpretentious speaker. Let me remind you of the line attributed to Mark Twain: 'It takes three weeks to write and perfect a good impromptu remark.' I believe that nobody is born a good speaker and that you have to work at your body language to *appear* relaxed and natural in the same way as Mark Twain worked on what appeared to be a throwaway line.

The perils of bad body language

If your inner panic shows itself in your fidgety feet and fiddling fingers, your audience will feel uncomfortable because they want and expect you to be in control. In addition, they will not have confidence in you, your ideas or your product or service. They will not believe in you, they won't listen well and will quickly forget what you have said. If you look confident and believe in yourself, you will have credibility and your listeners will be eager to hear what you have to say.

As you stand facing your audience, I don't think for one moment that you will feel cool, calm and confident – I expect you will be suffering anything from mild apprehension to abject terror, depending on the extent of your experience. At this stage don't worry about your *feelings* – for at this point you want simply to appear cool, calm and confident. The rest of this chapter shows you how you can achieve this.

Eye Communication

When I am training managers in effective speaking, I have to be very careful not to overrun my time when we reach the session on eye contact, because I am convinced that it is one of the most important factors towards creating a good speaker – and I love talking about the subject.

I could see it in his eyes

Looking at someone demonstrates that you are interested in them. Consider some of the common phrases about people in love: 'She only had eyes for him', 'They couldn't take their eyes off each other.' If you see two people standing together and talking, you can judge how intimate they are by observing the extent of their eye communication.

People can also use their eyes to give messages of disinterest. There is nothing more frustrating than trying to talk to someone at a party who is looking constantly over your shoulder and around the room.

Eye contact also denotes authority. Powerful people give more eye contact than those who are less confident.

We say that a person who avoids looking at us is 'shifty', but we also tell our children that staring is rude. Somewhere in between a shifty look and a stare is the correct eye contact, and it varies according to the degree of intimacy in our relationships. With eye contact, we can demonstrate our concern, love, dislike, boredom, disdain, even hatred – 'If looks could kill.' *We express our emotions through our eyes.*

Where is the audience?

I'm sure you have seen speakers who stare at the ceiling throughout their talk as if their script were written up there in large print. For variation they glance at the floor or out of the window to an imaginary listener sitting outside.

Some speakers follow the ludicrous advice, sometimes given to novice public speakers, to find a friendly face in the audience and speak to it. After a few minutes of continuous scrutiny, the poor victim in the audience is asking, why me? The rest of the audience is feeling excluded from what appears to be an exclusive monologue; finding a friendly face is unfair both to the 'face' and to the rest of the listeners present. Avoid speaking only to the most powerful or influential person present for the same reason.

Speakers tend to look at their notes, at the back of the room, at their visual aids or even at a blank flip chart – anywhere but at the audience.

Why is it difficult to look at the audience?

Before I answer that, let me ask you a question. Do you want your audience to know that you are feeling nervous? No, of course not, and that is the reason why you find it difficult to look at them. You know instinctively that you express your emotions through your eyes, so if you don't look at them, they won't be able to see how nervous you are.

Having people looking at you is unnerving, you feel put on the spot, cornered and trapped, so you distance yourself from the situation by looking out of the window. You feel, quite illogically, that if you don't look at them, they will be able to see less of you.

What happens when you don't make eye contact

People who are interested in each other make eye contact when they are talking because they want to know how their listener is receiving their message. When you don't look at the audience, they feel (probably unconsciously) that you are not interested in them, or in their reaction to your talk; they feel the same way as you do if someone at a party talks while looking over your shoulder; they feel you don't care whether they listen or not; and because they do not feel involved by you their concentration lags.

If you don't pay attention to your audience, they will not pay attention to you

This was demonstrated to me recently, when a speaker deliberately only made eye contact with half of his audience during a 40-minute presentation. It was a medium-sized group of 30 people and afterwards when they were asked to assess the speaker, half of them found him interesting, challenging and entertaining, and the other half found him uninspiring, boring and ineffective. You can guess what had made such a radical difference to their reaction.

How is your eye contact?

During the course of your everyday life, pay attention to the eye contact other people make with you, and try and note how easy or difficult you find it to look at people when you are talking in a variety of different situations. Ask friends for feedback on your own eye contact. Practise maintaining contact for longer than usual without it becoming uncomfortable.

How to overcome your reluctance to look at the audience

Here are some games to help you gain confidence when you are speaking.

Look around the group and check what colour your listeners' eyes are; how many are wearing glasses; do they have thick or thin eyebrows; do the eyebrows meet in the middle? Imagine you are looking through a one-way mirror and they can't see you. These games work with a relatively small group.

In a larger group you can look at noses or at foreheads and no one will realise that you are not looking at their eyes.

As your confidence grows, try to look at your audience's eyes and faces to see how they are reacting to your talk. In a larger group, you will need to follow a **W** or **M** shape through the audience with your eyes in order to look at every part of the hall or conference centre.

I have spoken from platforms where the bright lights aimed at the speakers made it impossible to see beyond the first row or so, but I know that it is not apparent to the audience that they are invisible, so I look out into blackness and move my eyes around as if I am looking at each person present.

What to avoid in eye contact

Once you have conquered your fear of looking at your listeners, you must improve the quality of your contact. Little, short, jerky glances are not good eye contact. Remember you are communicating your interest in your audience. Sweeping your eyes over people's faces will not convince them that you are seeking their reaction to your talk. Practise looking at each person for at least two to three seconds. If this is too difficult at first, practise on inanimate objects at home or in the office. Learn to gauge for yourself how long a 2-to-3-second eye rest is.

To check your eye contact after a talk, try to remember how each person looked – was the financial director frowning? Who smiled at your anecdotes? If you can recall their facial expressions, you were making good eye contact.

Facial Communication

Eye contact is essential, but if you are frowning or appear depressed, people will not believe that you are enjoying speaking to them. So, remember your 'I am happy' expression and if you have some difficulty raising a smile when you are suffering from nerves, look slowly at your audience one by one (this is particularly effective in a small group) and imagine that they are all sitting on the toilet!

When I was first promoting my company, Speak First, I met a number of rather pompous senior business people who made me feel unsure of myself and, on a couple of sales visits, I felt that I had not presented myself well because I had felt intimidated by them. On the next occasion, I wrote a note on the top of my pad to help myself to speak to the man and not be overawed by his position. I wrote 'think of him playing football in the nude, think of him playing with a toy duck in the bath'.

If you find yourself in a difficult situation where you fear your own feelings may hinder your performance, play a game to overcome your doubts. Think happy and avoid frowning at your listeners – it's not their fault that you feel nervous. You may have to exaggerate your smile if you are one of those people who can look rather sombre because, in repose, the corners of their mouths turn downwards.

Hands

When a speaker is fairly accomplished, it is often their hands that reveal apprehension.

What not to do with your hands

- *Fiddle* with rings, watch, cuff links, buttons, pens, elastic bands, paper-clips, spectacles, cuticles and nails, confidence cards, coins in pocket, pointers.

- *Touch and pat* face, hair, pockets, desk, table.

- *Clutch* back of chair, notes, side of lectern.

- *Scratch* any part of the body.

- *Hide them* behind back, in pockets, in lap, by folding arms, or by sitting on hands.

- *Point* at the audience.

- *Rub them together* in enthusiasm.

- *Wring them* in despair.

I am amazed at the range of activities that speakers find for their hands and I am sure that you have seen living examples of most of those that I have listed above.

What can you do with your hands?

Your hands do not have a separate identity – they are part of your arms and, in general, only need to move if you are making a gesture, and should only hold your confidence cards.

Arm gestures

You will see speakers making small gestures as if their arms were paralysed to the wrist or to the elbow. It is all part of the self-consciousness of being in front of an audience. Somehow they feel that if they make small gestures, they will not be quite so visible to the audience.

Remember your arm begins at your shoulder – always use all of your arm. Don't tuck in your elbows to your waist or make jerky, half-hearted, meaningless gestures. One of our trainers refers to this as Velcro elbows. I remember a tall woman on one of my courses who, through shyness, stood hunched up, making tiny movements with her hands. We advised her to stand tall, make eye contact and use her arms to express her enthusiasm. The result was startling – she became regal and was very impressive. Without even opening her mouth, she looked like a self-confident, interesting speaker.

When should you make gestures?

When you are not under stress, your gestures will coincide with what you are saying. You will use them to emphasise a point – 'I won't stand for this a moment longer'; you indicate a place – 'The management out there think that the staff . . .'; you can express an idea, a spiral staircase, or a size – 'We have an enormous majority . . .', 'The spare part we needed was expensive but very small.'

Some people naturally use more gestures than others; people from the Latin countries tend to use more gestures than those from northern Europe. These are natural gestures and you should continue to use them if this is your style. Under stress many people wave their arms in meaningless repetitive movements as if they were trying to shake off a persistent insect. Watch yourself on video if possible, or in front of a full-length mirror to check if you have any mannerisms you want to eliminate.

Useless gestures, as opposed to those with a purpose, reveal nervousness and become a distraction to the audience. Don't be afraid to use your arms, though, because standing rigid like a wooden soldier is as unnatural as waving your arms about unnecessarily.

What to do with your hands when you are not using your arms

Keep your hands empty and still by the sides of your body. This will feel odd, but it looks very natural. But don't keep your arms glued to your sides, because when a gesture is required, your hands will only make little waving movements somewhere down by your thighs.

Some speakers feel more comfortable with their hands held lightly in front of them at waist level – if you use this position, remember not to clench your hands together so they can't escape. If you do, your gestures will eventually show themselves through jerky elbow and shoulder movements.

Other speakers like to stand with their hands lightly clasped in what is known as the fig-leaf position, slightly below the waist. Once again, be sure that your hands are free to make gestures to suit the content of your talk.

If you are holding confidence cards, be sure to gesture with the other hand. Remember you can change hands so that you are able to use both during your talk.

Position and Posture

Avoiding barriers

Facing an audience, whether it is of five, 50 or 500, is difficult and speakers like to hide behind desks, tables or lecterns. If you want to be a good speaker, you must learn to stand totally exposed in front of your audience. Always stand in front of all the barriers.

Pitfalls of lecterns

I am 1.57m tall and some lecterns are 1.2m high, so how can I be a powerful speaker if my listeners can only see my head peeping over the edge? Even if you are over 1.8m tall, try to stand to one side of the lectern so that you can refer to your notes and your listeners can see all of your body. This will also make it easier for you to make natural gestures and to move around. If the lectern is fixed with a microphone, you have no choice but to stand behind it. Stand on a box if you are short so that your upper body can be seen. Ask for a radio microphone if you want to move away from the lectern.

Standing and sitting

I have referred to small meetings (about fifteen to twenty people) where it is customary to sit. If you can break this custom, do so, because standing gives you authority, enables you to breathe properly and project your voice, and to make better eye contact. The disadvantages of sitting are:

- your chest is restricted and it is difficult to use your lungs effectively;

- your eye contact may be limited and you may be tempted to look down at your notes too much;

- your listeners may not be able to see you;

- it will be very tempting to play with pens and paper-clips on the table.

The advantages of standing are:

- you are more visible and have more authority;

- your voice projection will be better;

- you will have room to make gestures (don't lean on the table or clutch the back of the chair if you are standing behind it).

Stand tall

Act confidently, even if you are quivering inside. If you could see yourself on video, you would be surprised at how little your nerves show. Push back your shoulders and open up your chest as if you are about to begin the first day of your holiday. Remember, if you look as if you believe in yourself, your listeners will accept and retain what you say. They are on your side, so don't disappoint them. Speak to them as if you find them extremely attractive and you expect them to like you.

Finding Your Feet

Like hands, these creatures on the ends of our legs seem to be stimulated by nerves to act very strangely. I have seen otherwise normal men and women:

- hopping from one foot to another;
- taking two steps forward and two steps back;
- standing on one leg;
- crossing their legs in the 'I want to go to the toilet' stance;
- rocking to and fro;
- swaying from side to side;
- flexing at the knees;
- rising up on their toes on every third word;
- rising up on their toes on every third word on a squeaky floorboard;
- sticking out one foot and 'boring for oil' with the heel;
- going on little, undirected walkabouts;
- tracking the pattern of the carpet with the curve of their shoe;
- walking up and down like a caged animal;
- standing on the sides of their shoes.

If you can identify any of these traits in your own performance, imagine that you are standing in weighted boots, so that it is impossible to move without a conscious decision. You should be aiming for steady, relevant movements, not cat-on-a-hot-tin-roof jerks. You don't have to stay nailed to one spot, but you should be consciously deciding when to move to another spot – to the flip chart, towards a questioner in the audience, to pick up a visual aid – and you should not be at the mercy of your fidgeting feet.

Sometimes I find speakers who have learnt to control their feet, but compensate by swinging their hips or swaying or even leaning to one side. Stand upright on two feet a few centimetres apart, so that your hips are balanced over them and your shoulders and the rest of your body are balanced over your hips. Don't slump or lean on one foot with your hip sticking out. Think of a core of calm confidence that is beaming out from the centre of your chest. Remember to follow the rules of body language listed in the summary overleaf and you are now in a position to open your mouth and begin to speak.

Silent Presentation

Finally, if you are part of a team presentation, there will be time both before and after your talk when you will be a silent presenter. In other words, you will be part of the presentation but as a listener.

It's essential that you look interested and tuned into your colleagues' talk. Now is not an appropriate moment to try either a last-minute mental rehearsal nor an anguished recall of what you left out during your turn at the lectern. This is especially important during pitches for new business; remember clients are assessing you as a team and your interaction (or lack of it) could be a significant factor in their decision.

SUMMARY

- Use your eyes to make contact with your audience and show that you are interested in their reaction to you.

- Your face should say, 'I am happy to be here and I'm glad you're here too.'

- Your hands should be empty and still.

- Gestures start from the shoulder.

- Don't hide behind barriers.

- Stand tall, don't sit.

- Balance on both feet and wear imaginary lead-weighted boots.

- Let the beam of calm confidence shine out from your chest.

11

Finding Your Voice

'His voice sounds a little as if he is eating biscuits'
MARIANNE MACDONALD (of Ian McKellan, *Observer* magazine,
March 1998)

There is no point in looking confident and feeling relaxed if your voice lets you down.

This is not a book about elocution and I am not a drama teacher, so don't expect me to show you how to develop a deep, melodious voice, throbbing with emotion, if you normally speak in a thin, squeaky voice. No matter how you sound, you probably dislike your own voice if you have ever heard it on a tape recorder. This chapter describes techniques to help you create a more interesting voice and avoid the faults common among inexperienced speakers.

Another Great Truth

Few people like the sound of their own voice. This is because throughout your life you have heard your voice through the bone of your jaw, while everyone else (including the tape recorder) hears it straight from your mouth. Hearing yourself on tape for the first time can be a shock, so try to be objective about it. However, if you feel your voice is a serious handicap, seek professional advice – either voice teacher or speech therapist. I can't hear you speak so I can't judge, but of all my clients I only recommend a small percentage to seek further help. For loss of voice on a regular basis (repeat infections), huskiness/croakiness, see your doctor to ask for a referral to an ENT (ear, nose and throat) consultant or speech therapist.

Accent

Bernard Shaw said that 'An Englishman has only to say one word for another to either admire him or despise him.' Indeed, the most common complaint people have about their voice is their accent: 'I sound so posh and stand-offish'; 'I sound so common'; 'I don't like the way I pronounce my Rs'; 'My accent makes me sound unintelligent'.

Regard your accent as part of your personality and only consider changing it if you cannot be understood. There are many examples of successful men and women who have made a feature of their accent: think of Ken Livingstone, Jonathan Ross, Jimmy Knapp and Janet Street-Porter, for example.

In the past few years major changes have occurred regarding regional accents. They have become more acceptable and even fashionable. Telephone call centres are manned by Scottish and Yorkshire voices; regional voices are part of our popular culture with radio and television personalities speaking in accents far removed from received pronunciation. Younger members of the royal family do not sound as if they have stepped out of a 1940s film like *Brief Encounter* and have dropped the clipped vowel sounds of Celia Johnson. Even compare the voice of Queen Elizabeth at her coronation with more recent recordings to hear the changes that have taken place.

Often voice coaches who are asked to change a client's voice find they only need to change their posture and breathing in order to achieve more clarity.

However, I should issue a word of warning to you if you have a strong regional accent. People whose mother tongue is not English may have difficulty understanding you. So, if you are speaking at an overseas conference, you will need to put on your 'posh' accent!

Volume, Clarity, Variety

To be an effective speaker you need:

- to be heard;

- to be understood;

- to have variety in your voice.

How to be heard

There are speakers whose soft voices make it difficult for their listeners to hear them, even in a small group. In addition there may be background noise – roadworks and traffic outside in the street, air conditioning or heating noise inside, as well as the general office hubbub in the adjoining rooms. After a while listeners give up straining to hear the quiet voice of the speaker and indulge in some internal conversations with themselves.

With larger audiences, you may have to speak over the sound of late-comers arriving, the rattle of china and cutlery, as well as coughing and nose blowing.

The secret of voice projection is to use your breath to support your voice as you speak from the stomach. If you exert pressure on your throat muscles to speak louder, your voice will sound strained and you will end up with a sore throat.

Breathe well to speak well

Most of us don't use our lungs well. In our everyday lives we take short, shallow breaths and only fill the top half of our lungs. Under stress we breathe more rapidly, and because we are not using the full capacity of our lungs, we become breathless; when we are speaking, we can even run out of air before we reach the end of a sentence.

The deeper you breathe, the more air you will have to sustain your voice and project it to all your listeners.

Try placing your hands on your ribs and feeling your lungs inflate. Now, take a deep breath and count aloud on that one breath. You should reach 30+ but don't cheat. Full lungs will enable you to finish long sentences with no ums or ers, will kill some of your panic and take the strain off your larynx, so that you will be able to project your voice like an opera singer.

Imagine that the air in your lungs is like water coming out of a garden hose; it can dribble out over the lawn or you can place your thumb over the end and direct it to the furthest corners of the garden. When you count out loud, control your air so that you can extend it for longer and longer. Each time you attempt this counting exercise, try to increase your breath control to reach a higher and higher number, and to extend your voice to the far corners of the room and beyond.

Projecting through a wall

Imagine that your voice is a laser beam and it can penetrate the wall into the next room. You will need lots of air to extend it in a controlled jet, past your voice box and unrestricted by your throat muscles and out through your mouth. Practise reading from this book into a tape recorder in your normal voice and then again projecting into the next room. You should be able to hear the difference as you use more air to carry your voice further and further. Remember not to force your voice – use the breath to support it. There is no excuse for not being heard.

If you suspect or have been told that you have a soft voice, practise using more air in your everyday conversation. At first it may feel unnatural and too loud, but persevere and you will find that people take more notice of you and interrupt you less. If you develop a strong voice, you will be perceived as someone who is worth listening to and you will have no trouble participating at meetings. Don't let your voice drop at the end of sentences, but maintain the same volume right to the final fullstop.

How to be understood

Many people speak with their teeth together, hardly moving their lips, and then wonder why they are not understood. I've said that you should be taking in air and there is no reason to keep it trapped behind your teeth. You don't have to save it. Let it out as you try this exercise. Say the alphabet out loud, opening your mouth wide as if you were talking through a half yawn, and imagine your jaws cannot close and your lips cannot touch, except on the letters B, M, P and W. Repeat the exercise using twice as much air and projecting into the next room; hold your pen in your hand between your lips to make sure they don't touch.

Try saying these sentences smoothly all on one breath, without pauses or jerkiness:

- 'No man would listen to you talk unless he knew that it was his turn next.'

- 'It is always the best policy to speak the truth, unless you are an exceptionally good liar.'

- 'One of the tests of leadership is the ability to recognise a problem before it becomes an emergency.'

Lost letters and swallowed sounds

Clarity and good diction don't mean changing your accent or personality, but do mean positively pronouncing every letter and sound in order to minimise the risk of being misunderstood. For example, 'Good morning' instead of 'G' morning'; 'little' instead of 'li'le'; and 'part of this market' instead of 'par o' dis mar'e'.

How to add variety

You should aim to add variety to your voice because even if the words of your talk are stimulating, if your voice doesn't sound exciting you will not have credibility and you won't keep your listeners' attention.

Some speakers have a naturally varied voice with plenty of 'colour', while others have to modify it consciously to sound more interesting. Nerves can often affect your voice and make it sound more monotone than normal. When assessing your own voice, don't rely only on a tape recorder, as it is difficult to listen objectively to how you sound. Ask colleagues for feedback on whether you need to improve the variety in your voice.

If you want to enliven your voice, you also need to vary:

- volume;

- speed; and

- pitch.

You also need to consider inflexion and emphasis (see below).

Volume

We have already looked at how you can learn to project your voice so that it can be heard and so that you sound more authoritative; now consider the power you have to vary the volume. Lower it if you have an important point you want to emphasise: 'Now, I am going to reveal to you the extent of petty thieving in this company.' Raise it when you call for action: 'We cannot allow this practice to continue.' Allow yourself to be dramatic and vary your volume to add spice to your voice.

You may feel that this is totally inappropriate behaviour for the small group meetings you attend. Don't dismiss these suggestions immediately, but think of some of the men and women whom you consider to be interesting speakers – you'll find that without it being obvious, they are using a wide range of volume when they speak. I'm not asking you to sound like a great actor playing King Lear or Lady Macbeth, but I am drawing your attention to the importance of *varying* your volume in order to avoid speaking in a dull, flat voice.

Speed

Clients often find that although they time their speeches when preparing for our training room exercises, when they present them in the group, they finish too early. This is because nerves affect their delivery and they talk more quickly. Learn to slow down. Speak at half the speed you think is correct and you will be understood better. Your words will be clearer and you will feel more in control. You can add power to your talk by slowing down and using pauses to indicate a change of subject and for emphasis.

Pauses mean power

You should slow down between words and between ideas. Remember how difficult it is for the listener to follow the spoken word, so make it easier for them by pausing when you are moving from one point to another. Novice speakers find pausing one of the most difficult techniques to acquire, but it is a very effective means of holding your audience's attention.

Use the pause to add emphasis to your words: 'We are facing

a very dangerous period in the history of the company [pause] very dangerous [pause, and look around with good eye contact], but the solution is here in this room [pause] in your hands.'

Silent pauses

Pauses are powerful only if they are silent. Speakers who can't bear silence fill it with the noise of their brain working as they search for the exact words. When their brain gets into gear, it emits the sound of 'er' and 'um' and 'mm' – non-words that convey nothing and distract listeners. Learn to think silently. In your everyday conversation, you may find that you are using other non-words such as 'I mean', 'basically', 'you know', 'actually' and 'you know what I mean', etc., so try to eliminate them completely as they are unnecessary and indicate a lack of concentration on your part. Sharpen up your conversation and eventually you will be sufficiently confident to pause when you are speaking in public.

Earlier in this book, I said that our brains process words at 500 words a minute and listeners can be easily distracted by their own thoughts because you are talking at only 150 words a minute. This difference between brain and speaking speeds works to your advantage when you are searching for a word. What you imagine to be a full half-minute's silence in your talk, is actually only a second or two, and is totally unnoticed by your audience. Time and time again on our courses, clients see themselves on video and are amazed that 'that terrible silence when I lost myself completely' turns out to be a passing moment. Remember, a pause is a compliment to the audience. You are showing you want to express yourself well and are taking time to choose the right words. No one expects you to be as word perfect as an actor – on the contrary, that might seem insincere – but neither do they want to hear your brain crashing through its gears with 'ers' and 'ums'.

Varying your speed

As well as using pauses, you must learn to change the speed of your delivery to add variety. Giving introductory background information and setting the scene for your subject may contain information with which most of the audience is familiar, therefore your delivery can be faster than that which you would use when you reach the main thrust of your argument.

When I referred to volume, I mentioned the dramatic effect of lowering your voice and also of using the full range from loud to soft; this can be combined with speed to make a memorable impact. Use a slow delivery and a low, soft voice (still audible) to capture the audience's attention.

Adding highs and lows

Many speakers find that nerves cause their voice to go up a few notes. Research shows that lower voices are more believable, so if you want to pitch yours lower you can practise the following exercise. Imagine you have a large Chinese gong and you are beating it, bong, bong, bong. Say out aloud the words 'Chinese gong, Chinese gong, gong, gong, bong, bong'. On each 'ong' sound, elongate the sound so that you can feel the vibrations in your throat. If you practise saying this for 2 minutes every morning and evening, your voice will be permanently lowered for as long as you keep up the exercise. You can test this out with a tape recorder. Speak into it before doing the exercises and again afterwards and you will hear that your voice has become lower.

However, you need highs as well as lows so that you avoid speaking in a monotone. Allow it to go up as you ask rhetorical questions, e.g. 'How can we show we care?'

Inflexion

Here is an opportunity to practise using the full range of your voice by saying the word 'really' to indicate the feelings expressed below:

'I have just lost my job.'   'Really?' (horror)
'You need to get your hair cut.'   'Really.' (annoyance)
'Your work is exceptionally good.' 'Really.' (pleasure)
'We will be finishing on time.'   'Really.' (disbelief)
'Truly I am looking forward to   'Really.' (sarcasm)
   working for him.'

Even a simple word like 'Hello' can indicate a variety of emotions by changing the inflexion.

'Hello' (pleased to see friends)
'Hello' (male welcoming a female friend)
'Hello' (surprised and delighted)

Notice as you say each of these 'Hellos' that the inflexion to show the feeling is always on the vowel sound. Therefore, if you want to give colour to your voice you should e-lon-gate the vowels. Try saying the following sentence 'I want to stay here for ever and ever' as 'I waaant to staaay heeere for eeeever and eeeever.'

Using Emphasis

Try giving a different meaning to the following sentence by emphasising a different word each time you read it 'Are you coming with me?' Emphasising the important words in your talk will help the listener and add variety and colour to your voice.

You can enhance the quality of the word, e.g. 'I am

delighted to hear your good news'; 'I was so *sorry* to hear he had died.'

With emphasis, you can put energy into your words. Try combining it with pausing. For example, 'He was [pause] a great leader.'

Further Exercises

I have mentioned the components of an interesting voice, but simply reading about them will not improve your delivery.

You need to *practise.* If you do not have the opportunity to practise your speaking in public as much as you would like, or if you prefer to do so outside your own working environment, consider joining a speaking club that offers you the possibility of learning to present your views in an interesting and persuasive manner. At most of them, the members come from a variety of backgrounds with the common purpose of practising their speaking skills. Each speaker is assessed following his assignment, a prepared speech or spontaneous talk, say, so that he receives instant feedback on his performance to enable him to improve.

I advise my clients to read aloud. Try reading a book to your children, or read a passage from the newspaper into a tape recorder to learn how to add variety, colour and drama to your voice. To be a convincing speaker, you need the magical quality of enthusiasm. Although it may be bubbling away inside you, if your voice doesn't express it, your audience won't be able to share it with you.

Articulation – the clarity of the words

You should aim to make the consonants clear and precise – consonants carry the meaning of the language, while vowels carry the sound. In order to make the consonants clear the organs making the consonant sounds must be clear and precise in their movements; the organs are lips, tongue and soft palate, in combination with the teeth and hard palate.

Here are some useful exercises to help with clarity:

1. Loosen jaw – draw hands down face and let jaw relax easily.

2. Open and close mouth easily as you repeat FAH FAH FAH FAH. BLAH BLAH

3. For loosening jaw say SAH KAH SHE FAH RAH – PAH KAH SHE FAH RAH – WAH KAH SHE FAH RAH – BAH KAH SHE FAH RAH – DAH KAH SHE FAH RAH.

4. Loosening lips WWW WWW WWW BBB BBB BBB WBW WBW WBW.

5. Loosening tongue, tongue tip to behind upper teeth and then to behind lower teeth (keep jaw open and still) – LLD DDD LLL DDD LDL LDL LDL.

6. Combination loosening – LLL LDL WWW LDL WLWD

7. Phrases for precise articulation: 'The tip of the tongue, the teeth and the lips'; 'Lah lee bo lee. zip e do da'; 'Repetition, repetition, repetition'; 'Whenever the weather is cold, whenever the weather is hot'; 'We'll weather the weather whatever the weather whether we like it or not.'

Variety

Variety in the voice can be achieved by variation in volume, pitch, speed and pause.

These exercises are designed to increase awareness of your own speech rhythm and sound pattern. Speak them aloud, varying your volume, pitch and speed.

EXERCISE 1 **Volume**

Loud, louder, shout, quiet, quietest, whisper, silence.
Crash, bang, clatter, smash. Hush, plush, slush.
Creep, peep, asleep. Hit, bit, grit.

EXERCISE 2 **Pitch**

Centre, high, low, deep, deepest, highest.
Up and down, awake, asleep, sky-high, ocean-deep.

When I sing the note gets higher and higher and higher.
When I speak the pitch gets lower and lower and lower.

In order to avoid a continuing downward inflection, don't start
a sentence on the finishing note of the previous sentence.

EXERCISE 3 **Speed**

Fast, faster, fastest, quick, lightning, flash, slow, slower, cease.
Run, jump, leap, stop, slink, drawl, crawl, elongate, lengthen,
hiss, buzz, jab, insinuate, prod, glide, float, dream.

The lion gave a sudden stop.
He let the dainty morsel drop,
And slunk reluctant to his cage,
Snarling with disappointed rage.

EXERCISE 4 **Pause**

Vary the time lapse between the following words:
Start.stop..begin.end....commence...cease..go...stop.resume......
desist.continue.refrain

Exercise 5   **Reading aloud**

'He came into the room, looked at the disorder and was perplexed. How it came to be like this he could not imagine. The silence was unbroken. He waited anxiously for some sign of life. Nothing at all. His eye moved furtively from wall to door, from floor to ... corner ... There in the corner, slumped between overturned chairs was a man, face drained to a pallor, and still as a lifeless creature. There was no phone in the house, no means of contact with the outside world. There was nothing to be done but to leave immediately and run, run as fast as he could away from the disorder, away from the chaos, away from responsibility. Tell no one, tell no one, get away, far away, run, run, fast, faster, faster: feet moving, feet, feet, feet, feet ... out of step, not my step; step, other step, louder, nearer, quicker, thus, thud. Stop.'

Voice Care

Do:

- drink plenty of water;

- inhale steam;

- reduce tea and coffee consumption (caffeine and alcohol are drying agents);

- stop smoking – and avoid smoky atmospheres;

- avoid throat clearing (bite your tongue – gently! – to generate saliva, swallow or take a sip of water);

- rest your voice each day.

Don't:

- force your voice over noise;

- push a tired voice;

- talk or whisper with an infected larynx;
- drink alcohol before speaking – however tempting!

Breathing and voice exercises

Breathing is fundamental to life. Although it is involuntary, most of use less than 10 per cent of our lungs' true capacity. Through deep breathing, we can greatly enhance our vocal performance.

EXERCISE 1   **Vacuuming the lungs** (breathing properly)

Breathe out all the air in your lungs. When you think they are empty, purse your lips and give an extra squeeze from the stomach. Close your mouth and pinch your nostrils together. When you feel blue and think you are about to collapse, simply release your fingers from your nose. Do not open your mouth or try to breathe in any way. Automatically the cold air will hit a spot deep in the pit of your stomach. This is the spot you should aim for when breathing deeply.

EXERCISE 2   **Panting** (build breath endurance)

Take a deep breath, into the spot you identified in exercise 1. Be careful not to raise the shoulders. Use a mirror to check. Pant like a dog, very lightly. You should be able to feel the top of your diaphragm (the muscle just below your breastbone) quivering in and out as you pant. Sustain it for as long as you can. Try to build gradually to 30 seconds and then 1 minute.

EXERCISE 3   **Counting by numbers** (breath control)

In this exercise it is important to keep a steady counting rhythm going. If you can borrow a metronome, set it to about

70–80 beats per minute to keep time. Alternatively, this is a good exercise to do while walking outside. Each step is one count. Take a good breath in to a count of four. Count aloud to four, then exhale silently to a count of four. Repeat four times. Breathe in to four, count to eight then exhale over eight beats. Repeat four times. Breathe in to four, count to twelve, exhale to a count of eight. Repeat four times.

EXERCISE 4 **Choo choo train** (breathing strength)

Take a good breath and hiss loudly until your breath is expelled. Practise hissing in short and long bursts varying the patterns. With practice, see if you can lengthen the exhalation while hissing to 25 or 30 seconds

EXERCISE 5 **ha, HA, HA!** (volume)

Choose a point close to you in the room. It could be the corner of a table, or a door handle. Take a good breath and say 'ha' to the point and imagine the sound comes back to you in a straight line. Pick a point further away, say 3–4 metres. Say 'HA' to this point in the same way. Finally, concentrate on the furthest point in the room from where you are standing, say 'HA!' in the same way, and 'feel' the sound return to you along the same line it went. Practise this a few times, and you should feel the kick in your diaphragm increase as you say 'ha' each time. Keep going until you can definitely feel the difference in the volume you need to hit each point.

EXERCISE 6 **One to ten** (voice projection)

Take a good breath. Count to ten aloud, slowly, starting in a whisper and building up the volume so that it is loudest when you reach ten. Repeat, but be careful that the pitch (level) of the voice does not rise as you get louder. Concentrate on keeping it at the same level as the volume increases.

EXERCISE 7 **Hickory dickory** (lowering a high voice)

This one is good for lowering high voices (particularly female), which tend to be worse when we are nervous. Stand up straight and take a good breath. Start saying the nursery rhyme 'Hickory Dickory Dock', bending forward from the waist as you do so. You should be bent over so that your upper body is parallel to the floor as you reach the word 'clock' and you should notice a slight drop in pitch. Continue the rhyme and unbend as you do so, listening carefully so as not to let the pitch slip up again. Now repeat the rhyme in this lower pitch, without bending over. Try with other nursery rhymes for variation!

EXERCISE 8 **The bells** (varying tone)

Stand tall and take a good breath. Say (in a sing-song voice) 'bing bong' in the highest voice you can, immediately followed by 'ding dong' in a medium-pitched voice, and then 'king kong' in the lowest voice possible. As you do so, put your right hand above your head, at shoulder height and then dropped down by your side respectively. Repeat until the changes between the registers are smooth.

EXERCISE 9 **Roller-coaster** (varying pitch)

Say nursery rhymes (or any sentences) aloud as if you are creating a roller-coaster with your voice. Go from high to low in sweeping movements, and practise different words on different pitches each time. Do this for about 2 minutes at a time, rest for one then repeat.

EXERCISE 10 **The articulators** (clear articulation)

Say in a clear voice 'The tip of the tongue, the teeth and the lips.' These are what we call the articulators. They form the consonants that make our words understandable. Make sure when you say this sentence that you pay particular attention to the 'd' of the an**d**. Practise at varying speeds and different volumes.

EXERCISE 11 **Tongue twisters** (improving articulation)

Say your favourite tongue twisters, concentrating on the ones you find the most difficult. Start slowly and build up speed. Practise at different volumes, paying special attention to the consonants at the ends of words. Here are a few to start you off:

A flea and fly got lost in a flute, said the fly let us flee, said the flea let us fly, so they flew through a flaw in the flute.

Red leather, yellow leather. (Repeat 6 times)

Peter Piper picked a peck of pickled peppers. If Peter Piper picked a peck of pickled peppers, where's the peck of pickled peppers Peter Piper picked?

A proper cup of coffee in a proper copper coffee pot.

SUMMARY

- Breath gives authority to your voice.
- Open your mouth for clarity.
- Vary the volume, speed and pitch.
- Silent pauses are powerful.

12

Using Humour Successfully

'Wit had truth in it; wisecracking is simply
callisthenics with words'
DOROTHY PARKER

Now that you're feeling more sure of yourself and have estab-
lished your voice, I'd like to look at the reasons for using
humour in your presentation and how to do it effectively. I
have to admit that I debated whether or not to write this
chapter, because I find the subject of humour difficult.
However, I suspect that you may feel the same and, for that
reason, I am including a few suggestions on how to make your
audience smile. The humour I am describing isn't intended to
provoke helpless laughter in your audience. If you *are* able to
achieve this and you feel it appropriate for a business presentation, you won't need to read the rest of this chapter.
Alternatively, you may feel uneasy about attempting to be
funny and you may worry that you will run the risk of ruining
a good talk by including what turns out to be an unamusing
witticism. If you feel like this, remember that there is no obli-
gation to be humorous. But, if you can do it successfully, there
are several advantages.

Why Include Humour?

Humour at the beginning of the presentation relaxes the audience and also eases the tension for you. Audiences, even a small group, sense the apprehension you feel as you stand to speak to them and they want to be reassured that they are in good hands. By giving them something to laugh at, you show that you are in control. Smiling and laughing together unites an audience and creates an atmosphere of listening together. An audience of local business people enjoyed this comment from a bank manager: 'It seems to me that many people look on a visit to their bank manager with the same dread as a visit to the dentist. Really we're not that bad.' You can establish a rapport with the audience by using humour so that they feel well disposed towards you, which is particularly important if you are selling ideas or products.

Humour is useful to lighten a heavy and possibly dull passage in your talk and to make it more digestible and therefore more memorable. Take a look at your own experience, your own background and the subject area you're talking about to find stories that are funny and prompt a small smile of recognition on people's faces. You can also use humour to illustrate major points or the transition between them.

What is Humour?

The humour that is suitable for a business presentation is difficult to classify, but it may be helpful to describe what it is not. Jokes are risky because they require a positive reaction from the audience, and if it's not forthcoming, it is obvious that the joke has flopped. A joke that fails to raise a smile causes embarrassment for you and for the audience, and has the opposite effect to the one that you intended. Professional comedians will tell you that audiences vary enormously and a joke that was successful one night may not even raise a titter on another. Ask yourself if you can afford to misjudge what will be an acceptable joke for your audience. Even when your joke is pertinent, you may ruin its effect by incorrect timing, emphasising the wrong word or, worse still, getting the punchline muddled up. You maybe a proficient joke teller within your group of friends, but it takes a special talent to deliver a joke successfully to larger audiences. My advice is to avoid them. There are other ways of including humour in your talk which don't require such a positive and therefore obvious reaction from the audience, and which, if unsuccessful, will not cause embarrassment to you or the audience.

The safest target for your humour is yourself. Show them your weaknesses and admit your failings. Tell stories against yourself. For instance, I remember the occasion when, as a guest speaker at a luncheon, I was waiting to be introduced. The chairman turned to me and asked if I was ready to begin and unfortunately added, 'Or shall we allow them to enjoy themselves a little longer?'

You may find that some of the best humour arises out of the situation, so don't be self-conscious about voicing a comment if it springs to mind. But never use the words, 'That reminds me of a story about . . .' because the tale that follows is usually irrelevant.

If you intend using humour in your talk to make people smile, you must know how to identify shared experiences and problems. Your humour must be relevant to the audience and should help to show that you are one of them or that you understand their situation and are in sympathy with their point of view. Depending on whom you are addressing, the problems will be different. If you are talking to a group of managers, you may refer to the disorganised methods of their secretaries; alternatively, if you are addressing secretaries, you may want to comment on their disorganised bosses. A management audience will probably respond to a witty remark about coping with difficult staff and an audience of staff members will appreciate a remark criticising management.

Here is an example, which I heard at a nurses' convention, of a story that works well because the audience all shared the same view of doctors. A man arrives in heaven and is being shown around by St Peter. He sees wonderful accommodation, beautiful gardens, sunny weather, and so on. Everyone is very peaceful, polite and friendly until, waiting in a queue for lunch, the new arrival is suddenly pushed aside by a man in a white coat, who rushes to the head of the line, grabs his food and stomps over to a table by himself. 'Who is that?' the new arrival asked St Peter. 'Oh, that's God,' came the reply, 'but sometimes he thinks he's a doctor!'

If you are part of the group you are addressing, you will be in a position to know the experiences and problems that are common to all of you, and it will be appropriate for you to make a passing remark about the inedible canteen food or the chairman's notorious bad taste in ties. With other audiences you mustn't attempt to gatecrash with humour, as they will resent an outsider making disparaging remarks about their canteen or their chairman. You will be on safer ground if you stick to scapegoats like the Post Office, poor service from garages and banks, and the vagaries of the weather.

If you feel awkward being humorous, you must practise aloud so that it becomes more natural. Include a few casual and apparently off-the-cuff remarks that you can deliver in a relaxed and unforced manner. Often it's the delivery and timing that causes the audience to smile, so speak slowly and remember that a raised eyebrow or a quizzical look may help to show that you are making a light-hearted remark.

Look for the humour. It often comes from the unexpected. A twist on a familiar quote, 'If at first you don't succeed, give up', 'The darkest hour is just before you're overdrawn' or a play on words or on a situation. Search for exaggeration and understatements. Look at your talk and pick out a few words or sentences that you can turn about and inject with humour. In a serious presentation, an unexpected colloquial expression adds a light note; for instance 'an almighty cock-up' instead of 'a significant error'.

You'll also find humour in your everyday life. Look back to yesterday and you'll remember something that may not have seemed particularly funny at the time, but that would be so in retelling.

Build a Humour File

There are several books available purporting to contain humour and wit. I have listened to highly amusing speakers who have incorporated stories and anecdotes in their talks, which I know to have originated from these sources, but I think it takes a particularly discerning eye to recognise a funny story in print. The secret of employing what I call 'second-hand humour' is to personalise it so that it appears to be your own experience. Here's an example:

> A young man who was just about to embark on a business career went to see his grandfather, who had founded the family firm. 'Remember, my boy, that in business honesty is still the best policy.'
>
> 'Right, grandfather,' said the grandson.
>
> 'But before you do anything else, read up on company law,' recommended the old man. 'You would be surprised at the kinds of thing that you can do in the name of business and still be honest.'

You can modify this story by recalling the advice that your own father gave you when you started work: 'He told me that in business honesty is the best policy. He also advised me to read up on company law because, as he put it, "You'd be surprised at the kinds of thing you can do in the name of business and still be honest."'

Reading this story now you'll probably not find it particularly amusing, but remember that in the right context and with the appropriate audience it will provide a light-hearted moment.

If you are talking to a group of people you know well, you can substitute the name of a mutual colleague in order to personalise the story: 'I understand that Adam Sums, our new accountant, was asked by the managing director during his interview "What is ten times ten?" Apparently he made his mark by replying, "That rather depends on the figure you had in mind sir."'

Looking through books of humour is time-consuming and should only be undertaken in small chunks, as after a while nothing seems to be amusing. Try putting such books by the side of the lavatory or by your bed so that you can read a few stories at a time and judge them individually.

Keep a cuttings file of news about your industry or profession. You may find that you can link several incidents into a humorous story. Steal other people's ideas and anecdotes if they help to illustrate your point of view.

Keep a file of case histories, examples and stories you have found funny and feel you'll be able to use in future. You'll only be able to use it if you keep track of it. Ideas just fly away if you don't capture them on paper in such a way that you can find them when you need them.

Watch television programmes and crib from them. Many scripts are now available in book form and some one-liners are useful to add a sparkle to your talk. But be careful only to use material that is relevant to the audience. Also beware of sexist stories that will antagonise women, and avoid religious and racist comments.

If you do use material from a well-known personality you can preface your remarks by using his or her name. For example, 'On the subject of politicians, I agree with Clive Anderson when he said that they have a lot in common with chimpanzees – the higher they climb the more unpleasant features they reveal.' Incidentally this is a story that can be adapted to suit any audience or group of people by substituting the appropriate word for politicians. Here is another example, 'Bob Hope put it well when he described banks as places that will lend you money only if you can prove that you don't need it.'

How to Deliver a Humorous Line

Humour should never be announced: 'I must tell you an amusing thing my father said to me ...' This kills the story. Your wit must appear to be a spontaneous throw-away comment that the audience can choose to smile at. If you tell them beforehand that they will find it funny, they will be expecting an exceptionally good story. Unannounced humour makes the audience feel that they have individually recognised the fun side of your character. It's the difference between having a good meal in an unknown restaurant that you have personally discovered and having a good meal in a highly recommended restaurant. The first meal will be unexpected and therefore will seem better, even if it is not. The most successful humour is the unexpected peep behind the serious exterior. Your delivery mustn't indicate that you are telling an amusing story. A twinkle in your eye is more appealing than laughter and giggles at your own witticisms. Remember to slow down for the punchline and be careful to enunciate every word.

Beware of relying on an accent, dialect or funny voice to be amusing – you may find it difficult to reproduce it accurately under stress.

Never read anecdotes, humorous stories or jokes, as they'll sound artificial and forced. Your humour should appear to be spontaneous and uncontrived, and you can't achieve this naturalness if you are reading every word. You also need plenty of eye contact to judge how your humour is being received.

Timing is crucial if your humour is to succeed. This is a combination of pausing between words and sentences, and phrasing, which is grouping words together. Record one of your favourite comedians and analyse how he or she uses pauses effectively. Try to stress the important words. Pause after your humorous line, but quickly pick up the thread of your talk after the audience has reacted. If there is no response, don't agonise, simply continue in a calm, unruffled manner. Some of the audience may be smiling inside. You are not a comic and the success of your presentation doesn't depend on your ability to bring the house down. I know from experience that different audiences can respond differently to the same line and, if an expected smile doesn't materialise, you must carry on with the rest of your talk. I prefer to stick to one-liners because they can pass unnoticed if they don't succeed, and not throw you off course.

Inexperienced speakers will often swallow or mumble humorous remarks because they are concerned that they won't be considered funny by the audience. That's a sure-fire path to failure. Don't include humour if you feel uncomfortable about speaking out. You need courage and confidence to win a round of smiles.

Like all speaking, your humour must be researched and practised until you feel comfortable and familiar with it. Your body language and facial expressions, as well as your timing, are most important. Memorise your humorous lines so that you can look at your audience. Witty, light-hearted comments that are self-deprecating or which knock a common enemy are more effective than long, elaborate jokes. Aim to tickle the audience's mind.

SUMMARY

• Humour unites audiences.

• Use common problems and shared experiences.

• Avoid telling jokes.

• Collect funny stories.

• Never read your humorous lines.

• Aim for chuckles, not for belly laughs.

13

How to Handle Questions Effectively

'That's a good question for you to ask, not a wise question
for me to answer'
ANTHONY EDEN (to reporter in 1953, when asked what effect
Stalin's death might have on international affairs)

'Be sincere; be brief; be seated'
FRANKLIN D. ROOSEVELT

You've now carefully thought through your presentation – how you will look, what to say, how to say it, whether to use anecdotes, quotes or humour. But it is also important to prepare for what might happen at the end of your presentation.

Few presenters can get away without answering questions from their audience. You may even want to encourage an interactive style so that questions are asked and answered as they occur.

However, speakers frequently dread question time as they imagine they will be challenged and made to look foolish. There is only one way to prevent this from happening – anticipate and prepare. In this chapter I will describe techniques you can use so that you continue to project a confident presence throughout your question time.

When to Allow Questions

In a small group you may decide to allow questions through-out your presentation, as they occur naturally when they are most relevant. It's always a good idea to encourage questions if you are presenting an instructional talk as you'll need to check comprehension – and questions can provide valuable feedback for you.

I have said earlier in this book that I prefer to ask for questions to be kept until the end of my talk so that I can present my material in the order I have chosen, but when I am running training classes, I often pause for questions. This helps to maintain a higher level of concentration and allows the listeners to become active participants; questions also enable me to check that everyone has understood.

There are disadvantages to allowing questions during your presentation:

- they disrupt the flow and structure of your talk;

- the answer may be contained later on in your talk;

- only one person may be interested, i.e. the questioner.

You may be able to control a spontaneous question-and-answer session in a small informal group, but large audiences need to be managed more firmly. If you are the sole speaker, let the audience know when you expect questions and even suggest to them that they jot down those that occur to them as you are talking.

You should always schedule your questions before your final summing up so that you can end on a positive note. Don't forget that your last words to the audience will be retained longest and you don't want these to be a minor argument that you had with a questioner. When question time is over, if you have been unlucky enough to face any difficult or hostile questions, you should regain control by repeating your main points. Demonstrate to the audience that you are a reasonable person by finishing on a humorous note if this is appropriate.

When you restate your main proposition, include any comments from the audience that support it and ignore adverse questions or remarks. Thus, you show that you are confident and can cope calmly with controversy. The audience doesn't want to see you embarrassed and they expect you to behave in a professional manner.

If you are introduced by a chairperson, be sure to check beforehand who will handle the question-and-answer session. Unless you are part of a panel discussion, my preference is for the speaker to control the questions.

Questions to a Panel

On a panel it's advisable to allow questions immediately after each speaker, because if the audience has to wait until all the speakers have spoken, they will probably only be able to think of questions for the final speaker while the rest of the panel sit there looking superfluous. This happened to me at a conference where not a single question was directed to me, as I had spoken after lunch and the panel discussion was scheduled for the late afternoon. When the chairperson finally took pity on me and redirected a question, I was unable to answer as it was not within my field of experience. Panel questions are valuable, provided that the individual speakers have also had the opportunity to answer questions directly after their own talk.

How to Encourage Questions

• Tell the audience when you expect questions, i.e. during or at the end of your talk.

- Ask them to jot down any questions during the talk.

- Allow them enough time, at least 10 seconds, to change gear from being passive listeners to active participants.

- Plant a colleague in the audience to ask a question.

- Ask one yourself, such as 'You may be wondering why my company has come to specialise in this area; let me tell you ...'; 'I am sometimes asked about my personal background and you may be interested to know ...'

- Ask the audience a question. 'Did anyone disagree with the area of my talk dealing with the advertising budget, as I know that it is a contentious issue' or 'By a show of hands, could you indicate how many of you have used our services in the past?' And then direct a question to someone: 'Would you care to tell us of your experience, Sir?'

Too often speakers cannot tolerate the silence that follows when they ask for questions and they don't allow sufficient time for the audience to respond. Your body language should be alert and interested, but you can indicate that you consider the ball to be in their court by leaning back, maybe sipping some water and adopting a non-threatening listening stance. Above all, don't look anxious.

Rehearsing Questions and Answers

The question-and-answer session should also be rehearsed. There are some obvious advantages; practising helps you to:

- handle the unexpected;

- anticipate questions;

- field difficult questions;

- highlight weaknesses in your argument;

- expose ambiguity;

- answer questions using additional data.

How to rehearse

When you are closely involved with a subject, it's possible to arrive at a point where you are talking in your own shorthand and not fully explaining the logic of your arguments. This can be a particular danger when you are an expert talking to a 'lay' audience. Rehearsing your talk in front of colleagues and friends, and asking them to probe any areas that are not completely clear will help you to avoid this pitfall. If your actual audience has a high level of technical knowledge, try to find someone with a similar degree of understanding of the subject with whom you can rehearse.

When questions arise during your rehearsal period, analyse them and the reason why they have been posed. Is the question:

- relevant;

- referring to material that appears later in your talk;

- one that you want to practise answering for the question-and-answer session.

Ask yourself whether these questions have arisen because of a lack of clarity, too much detail, an illogical argument or simply because it is impossible to include everything and such a question can be answered at the end of your talk.

Often you can hint in your talk that you will explain further if anyone asks you to do so at the end of your talk: 'As you know we decided not to increase our exports to the USA this year and if anyone would like me to explain further on the reasons for this, please ask me at the end of my presentation.'

When you have discovered most of the areas you think may

provoke questions, prepare your answers carefully, including additional research into data you may not have had time for in your talk. You will feel more confident if you know that you have fresh, supplementary material to support your case. Be sure to take it with you in a form that is easily accessible during what may be a stressful time. You don't want to be seen shuffling through several files in your briefcase muttering 'I am sure I had it here somewhere . . .' If you are speaking to a small group, consider preparing an extra handout that outlines the additional evidence.

Look back to your mind map and re-evaluate some of the points you had to reject because of time constraints – might they form the basis of a question-and-answer session?

You may have omitted complex financial figures or technical analyses from your talk as they were inappropriate for the audience. But you may have to anticipate a question that requires you to provide more exact information.

Listen to the questions

Many inexperienced speakers find it difficult or impossible to handle questions because they fail to do one simple thing – they fail to listen to the question. So remember these points:

- Listen to the question – be sure that you understand it and, if not, ask the questioner to repeat or explain it.

- Make notes of the main points of the question.

- Ask for the questioner's name (and company if it's a public meeting), so that you can refer to them by name.

- Restate the question – this helps you and the rest of the audience to know what question you intend to answer.

- Answer it concisely – give your answer directly and, if necessary, supply statistics or use an illustration or even a personal experience to support it. Your audience has heard your speech, so don't give them another; make sure your answer is succinct.

Some Question-and-Answer Don'ts

• Don't be defensive. It's easy to feel that the questioner is your adversary, particularly when your subject is controversial. Be calm and polite as you acknowledge the questioner 'I am sure that many people will be glad you asked that question . . .'

• Don't rush to answer the question. Allow a pause as you consider the full implication of the question and how you can best answer it.

• Don't bluff. If you don't know the answer, say so (see below).

• Don't embarrass the questioner. 'I've already answered that but you obviously weren't listening.' Instead say something like 'I'm sorry I didn't explain that clearly.'

• Don't get into a dialogue with one questioner. If she insists on asking a supplementary question, answer it briefly and then break eye contact. Look towards the other side of the table or hall and indicate that there is another question. Suggest that, as there are several more questioners, you could discuss her question in more detail after your talk. If a senior manager is monopolising question time, you can ask him if you could answer other questioners and return to him afterwards. Remember you should aim to stay in control of the situation. (Also see How to Stop Ramblers below.)

• Don't answer questions that aren't relevant or interesting to the audience. I have witnessed a tax expert who was giving general information on taxation for small businesses become embroiled in a detailed question from one member of the audience. He should have suggested that it was inappropriate to discuss one individual case, instead of attempting to answer a personal question that was more suitable for a private discussion.

What to Say if You Don't Know the Answer

No one likes to admit their ignorance and if you are the expert who has just presented a successful talk, it is even more difficult. I am afraid you are going to have to bite the bullet. To help you, imagine that there is someone in the audience who is longing to expose your weakness. So far your presentation has been excellent, but suddenly he hears you giving wrong information – you are bluffing – up he jumps, at last he has caught you!

So, what can you do if you can't answer a question? Simply admit you don't know, and say you will find out and give the questioner the information when you have had time to do the necessary research. (If it is a large meeting, ask the questioner to leave name and telephone number with the chairperson.) Sometimes you can use the audience. Ask if anyone has had experience that could help the questioner. You can learn a great deal from the audience, and occasionally it won't be necessary to admit you don't know the answer. This is particularly useful in small groups.

I had a client whose boss delighted in throwing impossible questions at him at their monthly departmental meeting. My client was made to feel inadequate in front of his staff as he attempted to answer. We advised him to face his boss and ask him what questions he needed to prepare for for the meeting. This worked for a time until an unexpected question came flying across the room, but fortunately he felt courageous enough to say he didn't know as he hadn't prepared and that it required a detailed answer as it was such an expert question. From then on our client's boss seemed to have fewer questions.

How to Answer Difficult Questions

Hypothetical questions

They are generally prefixed with the words 'What *if* . . .' – 'So what happens if the new budget isn't approved?' Don't let yourself be drawn into 'doomsday' situations. Instead answer: 'We've spent two months preparing the new budget. It's a good budget and we're confident we'll get approval to put it into practice.' Politicians generally refuse to answer such questions and you can follow their example by saying that there is too much supposition in the question for you to give a sound answer.

Leading/loaded questions

'Surely you can see how unfair it is for the staff if we close the canteen during August? Why are you insisting on this?' If you don't challenge this first statement, it will appear that you agree with it. 'Everyone knows that this company is making vast profits, so what we want to know is why can't we have one more PC so that the work can be completed faster?' Remember once again to correct the first statement before you answer the question. 'I'd like to know why you think this company is making vast profits.' Here is another example: 'We know that you have found it difficult as the only woman on the board, dear, but do you feel you have achieved anything in your first year?' Don't be tempted to rise to the bait by saying 'Yes, I have found it very difficult and principally due to your pompous chauvinistic attitude.' Instead you need to change the word 'difficult'. 'Before I answer your question, may I just correct you on one point. I wouldn't describe my first year as difficult. I have found it stimulating and challenging, but above all very enjoyable.'

Off-the-record questions

Don't be fooled into thinking because you are addressing a small friendly group, you can speak candidly and in confidence. Answer all the questions 'on the record'.

The yes or no questions

This can appear to be very aggressive. 'Just answer yes or no. Is the pay increase agreed or not?' You don't have to limit your answer to yes or no – respond in your own words. 'I have considered the proposal for a pay increase from three angles and I think you should know what they are. First . . .'

'No win' questions

'Can you explain the decline in sales – is it due to poor management or poor selling?' Don't feel you must answer such a question with an 'either/or' answer. You could say: 'I prefer not to see it in such black and white terms as there are a number of important contributory factors.'

Useful Phrases

The cliché 'I am glad you asked me that' enables you to gain thinking time and you should develop a few more original phrases to help you organise your thoughts before and even during your answer. Here are some suggestions:

- 'To help me answer your question more accurately, could you tell me exactly why you are asking it?'

- 'I can see that you feel strongly about that and I admire you for saying so.'

Sometimes you will not want to answer a question, so you should think of how you can deflect it:

- 'We have spent some time on that problem/question, but what I think is more relevant to consider now is . . .'

- 'There is some merit in those points and it has been useful to hear from you but perhaps you are not aware that . . .'

How to Stop Ramblers

On occasion, you'll find that a questioner is unable to pose a question successfully and instead presents a long-winded rambling speech. What can you do?

- Use body language – hold up your hand and indicate that you want to answer the question if there is one. If not, simply give a brisk thank you and move on to another questioner.

- Highlight one part of the ramble and rephrase it in order to give a short answer.

- Use your voice to interrupt while explaining that time is running out and you can see that there are several other people who wish to ask questions.

These suggestions should be used with caution, particularly if the questioner could in any way affect your career prospects.

Handling Hecklers

Sometimes I am asked by a participant on a training course for techniques to handle hecklers. My usual reply is that people are extremely unlikely to be heckled during a business presentation. However, in case you are also curious, here are a few suggestions:

- Ignore the heckler and look in the opposite direction.

- Do *not* engage in a discussion with the heckler.

- Remember, the audience wants to hear you and is probably feeling embarrassed.

- Use a one liner slowly and loudly, e.g. 'It's good to hear your voice is working well – shame it's not connected to your brain' or 'Now there's a man with a ready wit [turn to the heckler], do let us know when it is ready.'

I hope that you won't find yourself in a situation where you will need to use any of these techniques.

Your Body Language During Question Time

Remember that your positive, confident stance shouldn't disappear when you stop talking and start taking questions. Listen intently to the question and, even if you think the questioner has totally failed to understand your argument, look pleasant.

As you begin to answer the questioner, look at him directly. However, if it's a fairly involved reply, look around and make eye contact with the rest of the audience and include them in your comments. You can also use expressions like 'I know this applies to many of you . . .' or 'I expect you'll find this useful . . .' so that they don't feel excluded. If you see that some people are nodding or appear to want more explanation, you can extend your answer after asking 'I can see several of you nodding; is this a problem that some of you have had to tackle already?'

If you feel under attack, don't allow your body language to reveal your unease – continue to look pleasant and confident as you search in your mind for suitable counter-arguments. I once saw a colleague being given a tough grilling so that afterwards he felt thoroughly exhausted. When I commented on how he had appeared confident and in total control, he said 'But you couldn't see my pounding heart.' He was right. Don't let yours show either – remember that people take you at face value, so keep looking poised.

SUMMARY

- Announce when you will answer questions, i.e. during or at the end of your talk.

- Plan a technique to encourage questions.

- Rehearse questions and answers.

- Don't bluff – admit ignorance.

- Use positive, pleasant body language.

14

Practising and Rehearsing

'The more I practise the luckier I get'
GARY PLAYER

Why Should You Practise?

There is no short cut to success and some experts in public
speaking recommend one hour of preparation for every minute
of presentation. Before you throw your hands up in horror,
remember that this includes your planning, organising and
developing stages as well as the practice.

No one ever allows enough time to practise and some of my
clients have a number of wonderful excuses why this should be
so – 'The information for the presentation was only ready the
night before', 'If I rehearse I get stale and I lack enthusiasm', 'I
know the material inside out', 'I don't want to look too slick',
and so on *ad infinitum*.

From my many years' experience of watching speakers, as
well as from presenting my own speeches, I know that rehearsing helps you to:

• become familiar with the flow of your material;

- conquer the blank mind syndrome;
- feel more confident and control nerves;
- develop an effective speaking voice;
- use positive and appropriate body language.

You are probably aware that practising is important and yet you keep putting it off until it is too late. I admit that I sometimes do the same and afterwards, when I have finished a presentation, I always wish that I had rehearsed more, because I know that I could have done it better. In reality, when you don't practise, you are using the audience as your rehearsal and that's not fair on them. You are not being fair on yourself either. You've probably spent sufficient time planning the content and choosing the words, but you fail to allocate enough time to what will make the difference between a mediocre and a memorable talk – practice. Remember, if you can get up an hour earlier you gain an extra hour in which to practise.

The Three-step Approach

Take it one step at a time – practice, rehearsal and dress rehearsal. Practising is done by yourself, rehearsing in front of one or several people and a dress rehearsal is on site with props. All your practising and rehearsing should be spoken aloud.

Guidelines

Your first run through will probably help you to add examples and even anecdotes that you hadn't thought of in your original preparation. I find that speaking out loud, even to an empty room, frees the brain to be more creative and so, although I have a full talk prepared at my first practice, I stop and make notes and amendments. Also, if you are reading it aloud for the first time, you may find that some sentences are too long or complicated, your choice of words may sound clumsy or you may feel some ideas could be expressed more clearly. It's tempting to continue to alter words and phrases throughout your rehearsing. You must set yourself a time limit for changes, otherwise you will always be rehearsing new material and the main purpose of your practice, to become familiar with your talk, will never be achieved.

Don't forget your body language

You're practising to familiarise yourself with the ideas in your talk and words that convey them: you are also practising your body language and your voice.

Always stand when you are practising, so that you can use gestures and become used to holding your cards. Look around the room as if you were making eye contact with the audience. A full-length mirror helps at this stage, although there is nothing to beat recording yourself on video. Don't dismiss this as impractical if you don't have your own camera. It is possible to hire one and, although not cheap, if you have an important business presentation to prepare, on which your reputation and that of your company rests, you should consider making such a worthwhile investment to help you improve your performance.

I know of one senior woman executive who changed her entire presentation after seeing herself on video because she realised that she was not conveying her message effectively. As she had begun practising well in advance of her 'performance' she had adequate time to do so: another reason for beginning your practice in plenty of time.

Using a tape recorder

If you can't video yourself, the next best thing is to record yourself on a tape recorder. Listen critically to your voice. Is it clear? Are you varying the pitch, volume and speed? Are you using powerful silent pauses or are you filling up the spaces with non-words? Above all, is there enthusiasm and vitality in your voice? Does it sound interesting? If not, analyse how you can improve it and practise again and again.

If you know that you will be addressing a large audience without the help of a microphone, place your tape recorder at the far side of the room and project your voice to it. Forget your inhibitions and your neighbours. Who cares if they think that your behaviour is strange; it's more important that you practise now and get it right, than worry about the neighbours and later make a fool of yourself in front of 100 people. Make sure you are not straining your voice. Remember if you have lungs full of air, your voice will carry further and you won't need to force it.

Rehearsing with feedback

At the stage where you can refine your presentation, a live audience is very useful. Use colleagues or friends, but be sure to give them the background to your talk – who the audience is, what they expect, what your objective is and what you hope to achieve. Only then can your rehearsal audience criticise your talk constructively. You will probably feel very self-conscious and embarrassed but don't give up, try to give your talk as if you had the proper audience in front of you. Make eye contact, use gestures and sound enthusiastic. Make sure they know that you want them to take the situation seriously and that it is important for you to have this opportunity to practise. Use your cards and if you lose your place, don't make any comment, simply continue as you would in front of a real audience; this will give you practice in overcoming fluffs. Encourage your rehearsal audience to ask questions as this will also be good practice for you. (See Chapter 13 How to Handle Questions Effectively.) They may want additional information on some aspect of your talk – if so, maybe your real audience would also benefit from a clearer explanation.

When you eventually receive their comments, accept them objectively. It's too easy to say 'Yes, but . . .' and make excuses for not listening to their views. Make notes of what is said to you and only look at them the following day, when there is less pressure on you and you can evaluate them dispassionately.

Remember that to profit from feedback you must accept criticism with an open mind. It may be irritating but consider what an oyster does with a grain of sand – you too can benefit from unpleasant criticism and use it to create a better talk. If you gather enough feedback, you'll end up with a valuable string of pearls.

Be sure to ask your audience to give you positive feedback as well. Not general praise, but specific instances of good performance – you need to know what to keep. In our courses, we insist that our tutors limit their recommendations to a maximum of three points at each feedback session otherwise the students are overwhelmed and unable to assimilate the training.

Guidelines for feedback

These are some questions your rehearsal audience can use in order to assess whether or not you are presenting a successful talk. You may want to add some of your own which are more pertinent or relevant to your subject matter and objective. You can also use this check list to evaluate your own talk.

Introduction

• Is the first sentence attention grabbing?

- Have you shown the benefit to the audience in listening to you?

- Have you shown why you are qualified to speak on this subject?

- Have you announced your structure?

- Have you revealed understanding and knowledge of the listeners' attitudes and possible problems in the first minute or two?

- Have you identified with the audience early on?

Body of talk

- Have you announced your first point clearly?

- Have you used facts, examples, anecdotes, comparisons and statistics to support your main points?

- Have you summarised regularly?

- Have you recapped on the previous point before moving on to the next one?

- Have you used rhetorical questions to guide your audience along your path?

- Have you avoided jargon and abbreviations?

- Have you used visual aids in order to explain complex material or to add interest at a dull moment?

- Are the links between each point clear and logical?

Conclusion

- Have you indicated that the end of your talk is coming?

- Have you summarised your key points?

- Have you asked for action?

• Have you ended on a high note?

Check your timing

Always time every practice so that you know whether you need to add or amend your talk. If you overrun on time, avoid what so many inexperienced speakers do – either ignore it and continue to the end of the talk or speak faster in order to include every precious point. Running over is a discourtesy to everyone and shows a lack of professionalism. Speaking faster means that your audience will not be able to follow and may stop listening. If you have too much material for the time *cut* or *condense*.

Write the timings on your cards, so that when you are delivering your talk, you will know how much time you have left at any given moment. This is particularly important with longer speeches or on the occasions when you have to deal with unexpected questions that use up the time allocated to your talk.

See your talk as an outline

As a final confidence booster, try giving your talk without your cards. Put them at the other end of the room and attempt a run through without them. If there are one or two stumbling blocks where you have to refer to them, do so, but continue again without them. This will give you the opportunity to see the talk as an outline or as a series of ideas. If you can visualise the shape, it's often more helpful than trying to remember all the detail. After all it's probable that you know the subject well, so it's the sequence of points or the logical structure that you need to have at your fingertips.

Dress rehearsals

Dress rehearsals take place on the site and with the visual aids that you intend using. Most of what I want to say about this type of rehearsal is included in Chapter 16 Visiting the Site, but let me give you one or two suggestions about 'dress'.

Try practising at home in front of the mirror or on video dressed in the clothes which you will be wearing for your presentation or talk. This is essential if your body language is to look natural. I have seen men and women casually try to put their hand in a pocket only to discover that their trousers or skirt are too tight and a relaxed gesture turns into a nervous struggle. Wearing the same clothes enables you to practise all your gestures and identify some of those you may want to eliminate. I have a silk scarf which I love wearing, but because it keeps slipping, I tend to retie it repeatedly. Fortunately a co-trainer told me how distracting he found this, particularly when I was giving a lecture on distracting mannerisms! Now I only wear that scarf with a brooch securely pinning it so that it cannot move.

Watch out for fingers fiddling with rings, cuff links, watches or constantly undoing jacket buttons. Keep your jacket fastened and don't fiddle with anything. Some men empty their pockets of everything in order to avoid fiddling, and this also helps to ensure their jacket sits smoothly. Wear the same shoes to practise in that you will for your talk. Are they comfortable, or are you likely to move from foot to foot because your shoes are pinching? Naturally you will make sure that your trousers have a sharp crease and your shoes are well polished. A speaker who stands in front of an audience in a badly ironed shirt, creased trousers and a jacket bulging over a large stomach does not help his presentation. A woman with a skirt that's a size too small, hair falling into her eyes and too much jewellery doesn't help her case either.

SUMMARY

- Make time to practise, aloud and standing up.

- Use gestures and vary your voice.

- Use a tape recorder and/or video camera.

- Practise in front of friends and colleagues and ask for feedback.

- Remember you are the most important visual aid to your talk. Make sure that even before you open your mouth the audience feels that you are an enthusiastic and interesting speaker.

PART THREE

Practicalities

15

Writing and Reading Scripts for Conferences

'Some passages write themselves – others become
a forest of barbed wire and balloons'
RT HON ENOCH POWELL MP

Earlier in this book I have suggested that using notes is more effective than reading from a script. However, there may be occasions when a script is essential; for instance large audio-visual conferences. You may choose to read from a paper script or from autocue; whichever method you use, your first step is a good script.

How to Write Spoken English

As I have been writing this book, I have been imagining you reading it – in fact, I have tried to imagine having a conversation with you. It may be one-sided but I wanted to talk to you, as I find it easier to talk than to write. You will have noticed that my style is informal. But, at first, I found it quite difficult to write like this, as I was inhibited by having a pen in my hand.

Unless you are a professional scriptwriter or playwright, it's probable that whenever you write, your words will be read and not listened to. Written English is what we are trained to write and you may find it difficult to adopt a different style when you have to write spoken English. If you have ever seen the transcript of someone talking naturally, you'll have noticed that the sentences are short and sometimes even unfinished; the vocabulary may appear repetitious while other words may be rarely used. You'll also see that many of the sentences are ungrammatical, although the speaker may be well educated. If you write a script that is grammatically correct, it may sound rather formal. For example, in answer to 'Who is it?' how many people say 'It is I'? Most will say 'It's me.' It may be grammatically correct to say 'For whom is that telephone call?' but most people will say 'Who's that phone call for?'

Use a *simple vocabulary*. It's not only grammar that changes when we write to speak, it's also the choice of words and the style of sentence. Undoubtedly, your written vocabulary is larger than your spoken vocabulary. However, if you employ words that are not in everyday use, although they may look right on the paper, they will sound artificial when spoken. Remember, you are not seeking to impress your audience with your academic knowledge – your objective should be to explain your ideas clearly and precisely, so that your audience understands immediately. Of course, if you normally use an extensive vocabulary in your everyday speech and you're sure that your audience will understand, you shouldn't feel inhibited in using it. If you have difficulty in pronouncing a word, don't use it, because under stress you'll stumble and appear uncomfortable.

Here is an example of written vocabulary: 'Successful script writers should ensure that they utilise a vocabulary that is comprehensible to a specific audience.' Translated into spoken English, this becomes: 'Make sure you only use words your audience understands.'

Short, simple sentences are best

Sentence structure can cause problems for novice scriptwriters as they tend to use too many conjunctions (like, and so, however, but, nevertheless, and so on) and not enough full stops. A useful exercise when you have finished writing your script is to go through it and cross out all conjunctions, and replace them with full stops. It may *look* wrong, but it will *sound* right. The best test of your script is to read it aloud. How does it sound? Would you really express yourself that way? Is it wordy and contrived? It should be natural and simple.

Always ensure that the main point comes at the beginning of your sentence, followed by any qualifying phrases. This is the exact reverse of correct written English. Here is an example of correct written English: 'Provided that our new warehouse is open in July and our sales for domestic appliances continue to grow in Germany, I am going to recommend that we expand our export drive to France.' Here is the same sentence translated into spoken English: 'I am going to recommend we expand our export drive to France. Of course that's provided that our new warehouse is open in July and our sales for domestic appliances continue to grow in Germany.' This sequence of ideas is important because as listeners we cannot hold qualifying phrases in suspension, waiting to hear the total sentence before we can understand the point. You may know what the end of your sentence is, but your listeners won't.

More pitfalls to avoid

When we compose written English, we often use the passive voice, for example, 'Hand movements are to be controlled by speakers when addressing an audience.' If you write like this in your script, it will sound academic and remote. Instead, use an active voice, for example, 'You should control your hand movements when you're addressing an audience.'

Remember that when we speak, we abbreviate words. Cannot becomes can't, would not becomes wouldn't. Make sure your script does not have any unabbreviated words or you will read them out and it will sound artificial. Have you ever heard speakers refer to the 'point above'? In spoken English this should be 'my last point' or 'the point I've just made'.

How to Type a Script

Here are some suggestions on the layout of your script that will make it easier to read. Remember that the lighting at the lectern may not be very bright and therefore your script must be clear and simple to read.

- Use a large typeface and use both upper and lower case.

- Use double or triple spaces between lines and twice that between paragraphs.

- Use wide margins.

- Only type on one side of the paper.

- Spell out numbers in words, for example, three thousand four hundred and fifty pounds and not £3,450.

- Don't continue a sentence from one page to another.

- Number each page.

- Don't staple pages together.

- Mark visual aids in the margin in colour.

Hints on Reading a Script

I have already described the disadvantages of reading a script, but there may be occasions when you can't avoid it. You may want to ensure that no essential points are omitted that could lead to misunderstanding, particularly if you are likely to be quoted by the press or when your words may be legally binding; you could be presenting a particularly sensitive policy statement or you may be making a speech for a political party.

Reading a paper

For some reason there is a tradition that scientific or technical papers are read. I find this discourteous to the audience as they have come to hear a talk and not a 'reading'. If you are presenting a paper at a conference or convention, you may also have to submit your speech in advance so that it can be given to the delegates in the conference folder. If this is the case, consider how you can enliven your presentation with additional new material – do you have any anecdotes or personal stories that might illustrate the main points of your talk? These might be unsuitable for inclusion in the paper that is distributed to the conference delegates, but they would add to the audience's enjoyment of your talk. Explain some of the problems you have encountered and any doubts that you may have had about resolving them. In this way, the audience is gaining from having come to listen to you; if you simply read a script to them, they might feel that they could have stayed at home and read it for themselves. Pay them the compliment of disclosing more of yourself than you might want to put into the paper.

Complex Audio-visual Productions

You will need to have a written script if you are reading your talk from a teleprompter. If you are involved in an elaborate production with slide presentations and video, you will be expected to give voice cues to the technician. He will be following your script and, as you reach certain words, he will activate the appropriate visual. It is possible to work without a script on this kind of production, but it can lead to mistakes such as the wrong visual appearing or visuals getting out of synchronisation. This looks unprofessional and loses credibility for the speaker.

Using a Teleprompter

A few years ago only TV presenters used teleprompters – often also called autocue (which is, in fact, a brand name). Then it was discovered by politicians and now it's not uncommon to find it in front of business speakers at conferences.

It consists of a one-way mirror (screen) placed in front of you and on to which your script is projected. The audience can see your face through the screen and, as you read the words on the screen, you appear to be looking through it at the audience. Your talk is prepared on a word processor and relayed by closed-circuit TV cameras through monitors near to the speaking point. From the monitor it's reflected on to the one-way mirror or screen in front of you. The operator, hidden from the audience, carefully follows the speed at which you are speaking and moves the roll of script.

Advantages of using a teleprompter

Using a teleprompter means that you can read your entire script and also maintain eye contact with the audience. With several display screens in appropriate positions, you can walk about and appear to be talking naturally with no notes or prompts. Even sophisticated audiences who recognise the display screens will quickly forget that they are being used once the speaker starts to talk.

If you use spectacles to read, you may find that you don't need them to read a teleprompter as the print is very large with

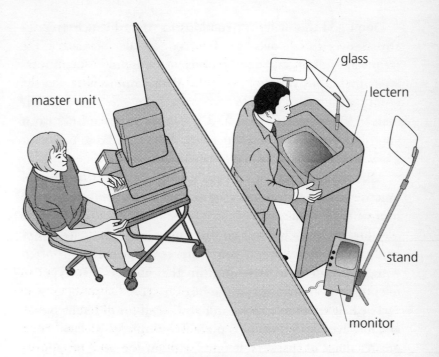

How a teleprompter works

only four words to the line. This is particularly helpful if you normally have the problem of having to take your spectacles off in order to look at the audience or to look at your notes.

How to use a teleprompter like a pro

Make sure your script is sent to the teleprompt company with enough time to make last-minute changes; when several speakers want to modify and amend their talks at the eleventh hour, there could be problems for the audio-visual production team. Remember that they operate from voice cues, so if you change your script you must reposition the cues to indicate when your visuals should be projected. Send your script approximately five to seven days before the date of your presentation so that it can be typed out for the teleprompt camera.

Don't add too many instructions to yourself, such as 'MD crosses over to left of stage. I introduce sales manager.' TV scripts are full of stage instructions and the professional overlooks them, but you will only find them confusing if you see them on the screen. The teleprompt display screen is approximately 300mm by 200mm and shows six to seven lines, so if you fill the screen with instructions, you will need to pause for a few moments before you continue speaking.

Ask for a copy of your script as it will appear, so that you can practise reading it aloud. It's useful to become familiar with the four words per line format.

Allow at least two full run-throughs with the teleprompt company at the venue of your conference or meeting. Often you will find that coaching in the use of this type of teleprompter is included in the hire charge.

The height of the screen can be adjusted for different speakers; however, if the screen is placed vertically, this allows for a greater range of speakers' heights without the need for adjustment.

Use at least two screens at each lectern to give you the flexibility to move your head more naturally from side to side.

Some teleprompter don'ts

- Don't stare at the screen – look away from time to time.

- Don't speak too quickly – the operator will move the script according to the speed of your delivery.

- Don't clutch the lectern – make appropriate hand gestures.

- Don't keep your head in a rigid position – relax and move it naturally.

- Don't frown – look pleasant and remember to smile!

How to make your script sound natural

I have suggested techniques you can follow to write a script in spoken English and not written English, but words alone will not convince your audience. Most of your impact must come from your voice and your visual appearance. Reading a script limits your body language, so you must rely on your voice to express enthusiasm and vitality. Few people are naturally good readers, but it is a skill you can learn through practice.

Final warning

If you have a good, natural script and you learn to use the teleprompter well, it can help you to be a better speaker, but you must allow sufficient time to become familiar with the technique. You have to learn to *read well*; but recognise that not everyone can do this and you may find that you feel more confident using another form of delivery.

Reading Aloud

If you have small children use them as an excuse to read aloud; they are an uncritical audience and will enjoy hearing the full range of your voice. This is an opportunity for you to experiment with exaggeration – loud and soft, fast and slow, high and low. Use the full repertoire of your vocal range.

If you do not have children you can still read aloud from the newspaper, from a book or from a play. Learn to read ahead a few words, look up at an imaginary audience and deliver those words. With practice you will feel less dependent on the text. The more eye contact you can make with the audience, the more they will listen.

Practise, practise, practise

Once you have the typed copy of your script, read it aloud straight through. You will find that there are many words that sound *awkward* and sentences that feel *clumsy*. Amend them so that they sound and feel comfortable for you. If you have the misfortune to have to read a script prepared by someone else you will need to allow extra time to personalise it. Don't feel that the scriptwriter is the expert and that the words are cast in stone. I have seen too many speakers stumbling their way through unfamiliar words and sentence constructions, embarrassing both the audience and themselves in the process. You must be the judge of what sounds natural for you. So modify, cut and add until you feel at ease with the script. But do put a time limit on making the changes or you will only have a final draft minutes before you are due to speak!

I was called to train a senior manager two days before an annual conference at which she was due to speak and although the script had been prepared for her, she had failed to find time to read it before our first training session. We spent several hours together, as I insisted she read and re-read the entire talk out loud. Eventually she was able to inject some colour into her voice as well as make some eye contact with the audience.

You don't need a speech consultant to sit with you. Save yourself money and use your own self-discipline to rehearse several times. But silent readings don't count; you must do it out loud.

Try these techniques

Practise reading ahead and raising your eyes as you say the last few words of each sentence. Look down, read the first few words of the next sentence, look up, and deliver them to your audience.

- Don't gabble because you have the full text in front of you – remember how effective pauses can be.

- Use your full voice repertoire – vary the speed and the pitch, use loud and soft for emphasis.

- Try to keep your head up so that your voice carries.

- Use facial expression to add impact to your talk.

- Don't turn over each page as you finish the last line; simply slide it across.

- If you need spectacles don't keep removing them during your speech. Use half-glasses and look over the top of them, simply letting your eyes come up and sweep over the rows of faces. Alternatively, you could try using contact lenses.

- Remember to arrange for a lectern on which you can rest your speech.

- Practise with a tape recorder or a video camera until you sound and look as if you are talking naturally.

Establishing Contact Before You Begin to Read

Reading a script may make you seem impersonal and remote, but you can reduce this effect by establishing contact with your audience before you begin reading. Start with a personal story you can deliver without referring to your script or involve the audience by asking them a question.

I began a talk on controlling nerves once by walking to the front of the stage and asking how many people would feel nervous in my position. Up shot the hands. Then I asked one or two of them to describe how they felt when they were nervous. Then I involved other people in the audience by asking whether they shared these symptoms. This short involving technique immediately raised the audience's interest level. Use a similar technique before you begin to read a script, and you will reveal more of yourself than you can when you are hidden behind a lectern.

Reading is a poor method of communicating your thoughts, but at least if you have a good script and can deliver it well, you have a better chance of keeping your listeners' attention. Finally, do remember what one wit said: 'Reading a script is like courting through a fence – you can hear every word but there's not a lot of contact.'

Check List for Conference Appearances

- *Introduction*   Make sure that the chairperson has a couple of paragraphs so that you can be introduced appropriately.

- *Delegates' pack*   If your paper or presentation is to be given to the delegates, make sure that the actual talk has different examples and anecdotes to bring it alive. You don't want the whole audience reading your script along with you.

- *Timing*   Always aim to speak for less time than your time slot; for a 20 minute slot aim for 15 minutes. Most speakers overrun in the heat of the moment and the conference organisers will be delighted if you underrun.

- *Other speakers*   Contact them in advance so that you don't overlap in your subject material. Also check that your clothes don't colour clash. It is advisable to find out the background colour of the stage setting for the same reason.

- *Microphones*   Find out what is being provided. Are they fixed on the lectern, or radio mikes with power packs?

- *Visual aids* How will the visuals be projected? Who has control of them? Are they operated by the speaker or by a technician?

- *Question time* Find out in advance how questions are going to be handled. Are they through a chairperson or will each speaker select questions from the floor? Will there be questions for individual speakers or a panel discussion at the end of each session?

- *Rehearsal* Check when you have entry to the venue and ensure that you have a complete run-through *in situ* with your visual aids and using the microphone. Practise crossing the stage if necessary from your seated position to the lectern.

- *Lights* Often you can't see the audience because of spotlights on your face. You may be able to ask for the house lights to be turned up so the audience is not in total darkness.

- *Audience* Mix with them before the talk if possible. Ask them what they are interested in. Encourage them to ask you questions at the end. If you can identify a few faces when you begin to speak, it will help to calm your nerves.

- *Speaking from a lectern* It is better to come out from behind the lectern if possible, even if only for a minute or two. In advance check that the audience can see more than the top of your head when you are behind the lectern.

- *Body language* The bigger the audience the bigger the gestures and facial expressions need to be.

- *Voice* With a slide presentation you will be looked at less so your voice has to be more interesting.

SUMMARY

- Don't worry excessively about the grammar.

- Use simple but precise words. And keep your sentences short.

- Abbreviate words like cannot, do not, should not, and so on.

- Read the script aloud several times to test its naturalness and until it is very familiar.

- Practise reading aloud from newspapers or from a book.

- Learn to read ahead and look up at the audience.

16

Visiting the Site

'Stop. Look. Listen.'
RALPH UPTON
(notice devised in 1912 for US railway crossings)

Whether you've planned to give your speech to delegates at a conference or a small gathering of your colleagues it is important to check out the venue for your presentation.

Where Are You Speaking?

Business talks are usually given in one of the following situations:

- round-the-table meetings on your own premises, for example, board meeting, sales meeting, departmental meeting, formal and informal;

- clients/customer meetings in your offices or on their premises, generally a group of less than twelve;

- regional meetings in hotels, such as a sales meeting with a medium-sized audience of 20 or more;

- conferences in hotels or conference centres with large audiences of over 150.

The Visit

Always attempt to visit the site where you will be talking, allowing sufficient time to change or rectify any details that might prevent you from presenting well and efficiently. I know that this is not always possible, if, say, you are in Edinburgh and your client is in Paris, but even if you see the room 10 minutes before the meeting is due to start, it will enable you to familiarise yourself with the layout and make minor changes. I am listing below the points that you should bear in mind when you are visiting sites of different sizes.

Small Venues

Check list for small venues

- Ask yourself how you want the audience sitting. Do they need tables? Would a semi-circle without tables facing the speaker be a better arrangement? Are there any members you want sitting together or separated or close to you? Can everyone see each other, you and the screen (if you arc using visual aids)?

- Is there adequate space for your notes, visual aids, handouts? Can you escape from the barrier of a table between you and the audience, or will you be trapped behind it? Where will you position your flip chart and projector?

- Where are the sockets for the equipment? Will you need an extension lead?

- How do you dim the lights if you need to? Is a pointer available to you to identify details on the screen? How can you adjust the heating or air conditioning? Can you open the windows?

- Who is providing tea/coffee and at what time? Imagine how your entire presentation could be jeopardised by the appearance of refreshments at a critical moment!

- Is there a clock in the room? Or should you take your own? It's often easier to read a small clock than your wristwatch, even if you remove it and place it in front of you.

- Who is providing pens, pads, drinking water?

- Is it to be a smoking or non-smoking meeting?

Dress rehearsal for small groups

You may feel that for a small group presentation a dress rehearsal is not necessary. However, I urge you to stand in the spot where you will be speaking and, at least once, rehearse out loud. This is particularly important if you are using visual aids, as you want to be sure that all the equipment works and that you feel confident using it.

In a small room, you should sit in all the seats to ensure the screen is visible from all positions. If possible, ask someone to take your place as speaker so that you can check you will not be obscuring the screen when you are addressing the group. I often find in such a group that I have to stand to one side when a visual is showing so that I am not in the way (read Chapters 5 and 6 on visual aids for more information on this). While rehearsing, move from the flip chart to the projector and across the area that is your 'stage' and check that no cables or junction boxes are in your path.

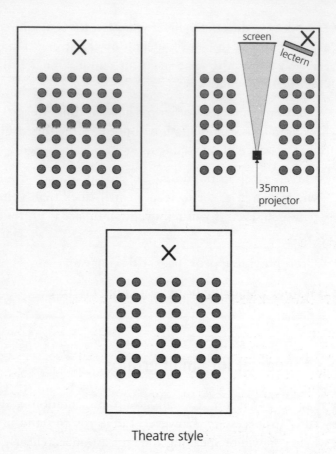

Theatre style

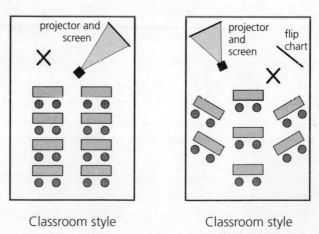

Classroom style   Classroom style

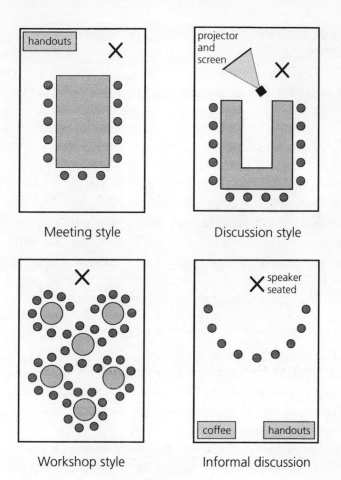

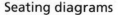

Seating diagrams

While you are rehearsing, remember to retime your talk on site and allow sufficient time for your audience to absorb the information contained in your visual aids. In a small group, there is a greater likelihood of interruptions and questions from your audience during your talk and therefore I suggest you plan to talk for 5 minutes less than your allocated slot so that you keep within the time limit.

Dress rehearsals for team presentations to clients

If you find it difficult to rehearse by yourself, it will take even greater discipline and courage to insist that those who are jointly presenting with you should rehearse as a team. I know how easy it is to outline roughly what each of you will do and casually reassure each other that it will be fine on the day. This is a big mistake. You should all have a very clear idea exactly what part of the presentation you will be covering, as well as how you will hand over to each other and whether one member can supply additional information if someone else omits it. I have seen terrible glares directed at someone who thought she was being helpful when she chipped in with an important point that the speaker had apparently forgotten. This kind of team support can be invaluable, but be sure to arrange between yourselves how it is to be handled, otherwise it can cause bad feeling. Make sure everyone understands their role and the framework in which they are speaking. This may sound too formal to you, but it can be handled in a manner that appears relaxed and casual, and allows everyone to be sure of what is expected of them.

I remember an unsuccessful presentation I made with another consultant at the beginning of my career in which he misinterpreted a sign from me and continued talking on all the points I was expecting to cover, thus resulting in a rather un-balanced presentation. We had been reluctant to rehearse together and we were sure we knew our stuff – we did, but we hadn't presented as a team before.

If you are working as part of a team, ensure that you have anticipated questions and planned answers, as well as deciding which member of the team should give them. In a sales presentation where your prospective clients are judging your company, a united team will go a long way to convincing them that you represent a reliable and successful company.

Medium-sized Venues

Check list for medium-sized venues

- Check everything on the list for small venues.

- If you are using a hotel, check the name of the manager in charge of hiring the room you are to use.

- What time will you be able to get into the room?

- Who will be in charge and who will be on duty?

- Are the chairs comfortable? Can they be substituted by better ones if your meeting is long? Ensure that surplus chairs will be removed. Remember to provide a seating layout plan.

- Make sure that no telephones in the meeting room will ring and disturb you.

- Ask to see the visual aids equipment. Are you familiar with the projector? Do you know how to focus this particular model? What type of screen will be provided? (See Chapters 5 and 6 on visual aids.)

- If you are using a lectern, how high is it? Can it be lowered or can they provide something for you to stand on if this is necessary? Does it have a light so that you can read your notes if the main lights are dimmed?

- Are you operating your own visual aids and, if not, what cues will you give to the technician?

- Check where the lighting switches are and who will operate them. Can only half the room be dimmed if necessary? Do the windows need to be covered?

- Where are the toilets and telephones; will you need a phonecard or loose change to make a call?

- What facilities does the hotel offer for taking messages?

- When and how will tea/coffee be served? Will it be served in the meeting room or in an adjacent room? If it is in the same room, ensure that the cups are laid out before the meeting. You don't want to give your talk to the accompaniment of rattling china.

Dress rehearsal for medium-sized groups

As the visual back-up becomes more elaborate and includes additional people, your technical dress rehearsal is even more important. You may not be in direct control of the visuals and the technician will be relying on you for a voice cue or a light cue (you press a button that flashes a light next to the technician). Your dress rehearsal should start at the point where you are first visible to the audience. Rehearse your entrance as well as stepping on to the platform. I remember seeing a woman in a tight skirt struggling to get on to the stage. This didn't make a good first impression. Some forethought could have prevented that. When you are introduced, walk purposefully to your speaking spot, pause, look at the audience, make eye contact and give them your 'I am happy' expression, take a good breath and then start to speak. That silence may feel long to you, but it allows the audience to focus on you and begin to listen. It shows them that you are in control. Novice speakers often start to speak too quickly and deliver in a high and rapid voice that lacks credibility and loses the audience's attention immediately.

Large Venues

For large conferences, most of the details should be organised by the conference co-ordinator. If that happens to be you, you will need to buy another book, because this is not the place to list everything you need to know. As a speaker your responsibility is to consider every aspect of your own talk and how you can ensure that your presentation will be professional and trouble free. Here are some points to consider:

Check list for large venues

- How will you approach the platform/stage?

- Where will you stand?

- Will there be other people on the stage with you?

- Is there a teleprompt?

- Can you see the audience or are the lights shining into your eyes?

- How are the visuals cued up?

- What type of microphone is provided? Is it fixed or will you be able to move around?

- Is the text of your talk being distributed to delegates and, if so, when?

Dress rehearsal for large groups

One of the most difficult performances I have ever given was in a large conference centre where half a dozen people were scattered about talking to one another and paying no attention to me. Occasionally doors opened and new people came in or shouted out obscure messages. Lights dimmed or suddenly brightened for no apparent reason, and visuals flashed on and off the screen. Through all this, I gave my presentation. Well, if you haven't guessed it already, I was at a dress rehearsal.

Very often they are disorganised but you should make the most of them because every moment of practice will help you to give a professional performance. Take the opportunity of practising your entrance as well as your introduction and your entire talk complete with cued visuals. If you are using a teleprompter for the first time, you will need some additional tuition. It is a knack to be able to use it well, but in order to be effective, you must practise several times. Don't rely on one dress rehearsal to get it right (see Chapter 15 Writing and Reading Scripts for Conferences).

Familiarity Breeds Confidence

These are probably the most important three words in this book and if you only follow this advice, you will become a better speaker.

Most of our worries about speaking in public are based on the fear that we will make a fool of ourselves, or worries about what people will think of us. We want the audience to respond and react and our biggest fear is that they won't. In fact it is unlikely that the audience will fail to respond, but in order to realise this, we need confidence.

Unfortunately you can't conjure confidence out of the air; it will only come with practice. Your audience will believe in you if you believe in yourself. Practising gives you confidence and enthusiasm – a winning formula.

SUMMARY

- Find out where you will be doing your presentation.

- Check the venue to make sure everything you need is there.

- Try to book time for a rehearsal at the site before the big day.

- Remember knowing about the site and its facilities will help you feel more confident.

17

Interaction With Your Audience

'Pretend everyone has a sign on their chest which reads –
"Make me feel important"'
TERRY PAULSON, American motivational speaker

I've said earlier that anyone who is listening to you is your audience, but obviously a large group of people behave differently from a group of five or six sitting informally in your office. As with visiting the site, there are different considerations depending on the size of the group you will be addressing.

No one listens with total concentration and anyone can be distracted by you, the speaker, as well as by their own internal thoughts. Now you need to consider the dynamics of the group and the interaction between the different members. I have divided up this section according to the size of the audience, whether small, medium or large.

Speaking to Small Groups

The interaction with a small group of between one and fifteen members is often visible. You should also be aware that in a meeting of several tiers of authority, such as managing director, marketing director and marketing manager, each person will be interpreting your message at two levels – their own, and how they imagine their boss and/or subordinates are receiving it. You have probably been in the situation where you have a good working relationship with one or two people and find that they act differently when joined by other colleagues. This is normal and shouldn't affect your presentation or talk. When I am making a presentation to, say, a board of directors, where I am friendly with one or two members, I speak with the same degree of formality to all of them, as it would be inappropriate for me to reveal our friendship.

You should bear in mind the personalities and relationships that exist within a group when you are presenting your ideas. Remember to maintain eye contact with everyone; it can be tempting only to look at a friendly face or at the most senior member whom you wish to impress and avoid looking at someone who you feel may disagree with you.

Discover personal barriers and relationships

Within your own company you will be aware of conflicts or liaisons that exist between people. Meetings with other companies, where you are not so familiar with the internal politics, can be more difficult. Use any contacts you already have to learn about your audience. It can be helpful to know of any quirks and personal likes and dislikes. For instance, the style of dress which is considered appropriate for a business presentation depends on the culture of the organisation. One of my clients, a creative and artistic film director, failed to obtain financial backing for a project because of his colourful shirt and casual suit. His bank manager didn't think he was serious enough to justify a loan. However, I have heard the story that Lord King, Chairman of British Airways, said of Richard Branson of Virgin, 'If he'd worn a suit, we would have taken him more seriously.' So it can work in your favour.

Find out as much as you can about the audience so that your message will be accepted and not rejected by their own personal barriers. Speaking to an unknown audience can be like crossing a minefield, but if you do your research you should be able to get through and deliver an effective talk.

Alternatively, you can set aside the first few minutes of your presentation to ask questions about the audience and their situation. All good sales people know the importance of listening and this is your opportunity to practise this skill; their answers will help you tailor your material to their needs. You don't need to change the core of your talk, but you can use the audience's experiences as examples.

At Speak First we always allow time for the participants to introduce themselves at the beginning of the course. I remember a student telling me her talks had been criticised for lacking structure so when we reached this stage in the training, I indicated to her that what we were suggesting would help her in the planning of future talks.

Find out: who will be there; their position and power; their relationship with each other; their attitude to your company and product/service; and any previous knowledge and experience of the subject of your talk.

Interpreting the body language of your audience and responding to it

In Chapter 10 How to Look Confident I emphasised the importance of eye contact, because an audience will stop listening if they feel you are not interested in them – looking at them shows that you are.

Watching the faces of your audience has another important advantage – it enables you to see how they are receiving what you are saying. In a small group this is particularly important because you can react to them. If someone is looking puzzled, you can check that they have understood: 'Ian, would you like me to expand on that point?' Someone may nod in agreement and you can involve them by saying, 'Sue, you look as if you have had some experience of that yourself.'

By placing their name at the beginning of your question, you alert them to the fact that you are talking directly to them and they can either decline or accept your invitation to speak. Be careful not to look surprised or disappointed if they don't respond, but simply continue with your talk. By speaking directly to them, you have involved them and shown your willingness to include them.

When someone is looking bored or uninterested, you can also ask them a question to allow them to express their thoughts, but if they do not answer, try not to be distracted by their lack of interest. I hate to see someone smothering a yawn, although I suppose an open yawn is worse. However, I have learnt to ignore it because although it may indicate boredom, it could also be totally unconnected with my talk – a sleepless night due to a sick child, a late night party or even a sign to the rest of the audience that the 'yawner' is superior and wants to distance herself from the meeting.

The non-verbal interaction between the members of the audience can also show you how your message is being received. Watch out for eye contact between them, as well as nods of agreement or negative signs like a shake of a head. Facial expression reveals much of what a person is thinking and feeling, but you should also pay attention to their bodies. For instance, sitting forward indicates more interest than sitting back.

You may feel that delivering a talk is difficult enough without closely watching and interpreting body language. In actual fact, I am sure that you are aware of all these signs already, but you may not have realised how you can use them to become a more effective speaker. Audiences want to feel they are important to the speaker and by acknowledging the signs they are giving you (sometimes unconsciously) you are paying them a compliment. (See also Chapter 18 Persuading, Selling and Convincing.)

Other involving techniques

Presenting to a small group is a challenge because you are
addressing individuals. You do need to break up your monologue to include them occasionally.

You can interpret their thoughts by watching their body language and involve them by directing a question to someone
who may have a personal contribution: 'John, I believe you've
had experience of this in your department, could you tell us a
little about it?' or 'Fiona, what particular problems have you
come up against using the old system?' In this way, you not
only enliven your talk with real-life examples, but you also give
the audience another voice to listen to, which will help to
extend their concentration span and allow you to speak for
longer.

Remember to build 'comprehension questions' into your
talk, so that you can check their understanding. Listen carefully to any comments or questions, but confine your answers
to the material you have already presented and don't be
tempted to reveal part of the rest of your talk. If you use
'comprehension questions' you will be involving the audience
but remaining in control of the situation.

How to cope with interruptions from the small audience

So much for the techniques of involving your audience, but
what do you do when the audience involves itself by interrupting? How can you deal with them? Try to remember that you
are in charge, that it is your show and that you should control
what happens.

Imagine that you are in full flow and a member of the audience asks a very relevant question. It is up to you to decide how
to handle the situation. If you feel that you can respond and
continue with your talk without a falter, do so. However, many

speakers are distracted by questions and find it difficult to resume their flow if they stop. If you are one of these, I suggest you lay down some ground rules before you begin speaking. Suggest that you would like to take questions at the end, but if anyone has difficulty following your talk, they should ask you to explain more fully.

The main advantage of keeping in control and not letting people interrupt you is that you stick to your predetermined structure, which you have designed to enable the audience to follow easily a logical sequence of points. Even if *you* have no problem in presenting your material in a haphazard manner in order to answer questions as they occur, your audience will be confused and may find it difficult to follow.

Chapter 13 How to Handle Questions Effectively deals more fully with handling questions, but you also need to be aware at this stage of the reasons why people ask questions.

Often it's because they want more information or don't understand a particular point. They may, however, see it as an opportunity to be controversial or witty in front of their boss or subordinates. If you suspect that this is the case, answer politely but don't allow yourself to be drawn into an argument or a discussion. You can remind the questioner that you have not finished your presentation and that you would like to return to the question at the end.

You may find yourself in a position of being unable to say 'I'll answer that later.' If your boss or a client asks you a question in the middle of your presentation, you may feel obliged to answer it. Do so using the minimum number of words and say that you find it easier to present the whole talk so that the questioner can see it in its entirety. I have seen a one-hour meeting spread over the whole afternoon because the speaker allowed himself to be interrupted. Remember, the concentration span of your audience is limited and if you don't keep control their minds will wander and your ideas will not be accepted or even remembered.

Speaking to Medium-sized Audiences

You will find that a group of more than 20 people has a different character from a smaller group, as each member loses some individuality and takes on the identity of the group. As a speaker your eye contact is more general and therefore the audience feels less involved; they may feel that there is less need for them to concentrate because they are less visible.

Think of how you feel in a group of five, of fifteen, of 50 and of 150 and you will see how an increased number of people changes the quality of the audience.

Interaction with the medium-sized audience

I consider a group of 20 to 30 as a medium-sized audience and you'll realise that you can't have the same personal interaction with each member as you can with a smaller group. Although you should certainly be aware of the audience's body language, you can only address that which appears to be most common: one person looking puzzled can be ignored (unless she is the most senior executive present), but half a dozen puzzled faces indicates that further explanations are necessary.

How to control the medium-sized audience

It is more important with a larger group to keep control as there is greater potential for disorganisation if you allow yourself to be side-tracked by spontaneous questions and comments. Do let them know that you want to keep interruptions to the minimum and, provided you smile when you say this, no one will take offence; if you tell them how valuable you know their time to be and that you don't want to waste it, you should find that they will co-operate.

Should you sit or stand?

Always stand if you possibly can. In some companies there is a tradition that speakers stay sitting and it takes a brave soul to break the convention. Try to be that brave soul. You will feel awkward and self-conscious to start with, but you will look and sound more powerful. Explain that you want to stand so that everyone can see you and so that your voice carries better.

You should not rest your hands on the table in front of you, but should stand tall and confidently project your voice to the furthest person (to overcome the sound of air conditioning, people coughing and shuffling papers, and so on) and maintain eye contact with as many people as possible. Remember to push your chair well back or even stand behind it and make sure your briefcase or handbag is not in the way of your feet. If possible stand without barriers – table or desk – between you and your audience. Your path to the flip chart or other visual aids should be clear, and if your handouts are to be distributed during the talk, ensure that they are in two or three central locations, so that this can be accomplished quickly and with little disruption.

To give a professional presentation and achieve your objectives, you must consider every small detail because you want the audience's attention focused on your talk and not on some minor distraction. Take a few minutes before you begin to speak to check the area around your feet for any obstacles and to check the space you have for hand and arm gestures; enthusiastic gestures are very effective provided they don't knock somebody on the head.

Include everyone with eye contact. By varying your gaze, you can avoid the tennis game effect – right, left; right, left.

Speaking to Large Audiences

When you can't see the whites of their eyes, you're addressing a large audience and entering the realm of public speaking. Individual eye contact is impossible except for those people in the first few rows, but you still need to look in the direction of as many people as possible. Remember to include other speakers and the chairperson who may be on the platform with you. Your body language should be more exaggerated and, in particular, be sure to smile more than in a smaller group as a person at the back of a big hall will be able to discern a proper smile, but will not see a small movement such as a raised eyebrow; a friendly expression is going to be more effective even when talking at a serious business conference.

Researching 200 people

You need to research a large audience as much as a smaller group. If you are speaking within your own company, you'll have no problem finding out what you need to know. However, if you are addressing a large group who have come independently to a public conference, you will need to address your questions to the organisers. Find out:

• how and why the audience is coming;

• what was written in the announcement of the conference;

• who else will be speaking and on what aspect of the topic;

See also 'Researching Your Audience' in Chapter 2.

I like to contact the other speakers by telephone to check that I will not overlap with their material. Also, if another woman is appearing, I ask what colour she'll be wearing so that my choice of outfit doesn't clash on the platform.

It always surprises me to see how speakers fail to chat to their audience at coffee breaks and meal times. I find these times an invaluable source of material and will often refer to a conversation I have had with a member of the audience before my talk. For example, I say, 'Someone was telling me during the coffee break that . . .' and this leads into my next point. It has the advantage of showing the audience that you are approachable and that you can relate to their problems and experiences. And you benefit from speaking face to face with the individuals who are your audience. It is also more relaxing than trying to fit in a final mental rehearsal.

Prepare for interruptions

At a formal conference there are fewer interruptions. However, you should plan how you would deal with any odd questions that may come in the middle of your speech.

Using common identity in large audiences

As a general rule it is more difficult to maintain a high degree of attention with a larger audience, because they are more likely to be distracted by their own thoughts and you can't use as much personal involvement. So, take advantage of the fact that they will act as a group in many instances. Laughter is infectious and an amusing story that might only raise a smile when told to an individual will get a more significant response from a larger audience. Humour is also a great unifier and if you can use it to relax the audience, they will appreciate you as a speaker. In large groups, if you can appeal to their common hopes and fears, their shared experiences, their admiration and contempt, they will respond to you. See also Chapter 12 Using Humour Successfully.

Understanding their concentration span

Audiences can only concentrate on one speaker for a limited period of time, after which they listen less attentively, and eventually become fidgety and bored. The concentration span depends on a number of factors:

- their initial interest in the subject;

- the time of day – people tend to be most attentive first thing in the morning and least attentive after lunch, particularly if they have been drinking alcohol. Speakers know this period as the Graveyard Slot;

- whether or not they think the speaker will expect them to answer a question;

- their own opinion and assessment of the speaker;

- their need to know about the subject.

Generally, an audience will concentrate most during the first 10 minutes of the talk and their interest will remain on a low plateau until they hear the words, 'Finally let me conclude by saying . . .'

From this you can see that you need to state your main message strongly at the beginning of the talk and repeat it at the end.

Ideally, one speaker should not talk for more than 20 minutes. I know that in many situations this is not practical, so I suggest a maximum of 40 minutes. If you need to speak for a longer period, consider splitting the time slot between two speakers. Be sure to work closely with one another, rehearsing together, and remember to plan ahead of time how you will deal with questions, so that you can give a united performance.

How to use interest prompts

There is frequently a low period in the middle of the concentration span and it's up to you to include interest prompts in your talk to keep the audience's attention. Here are some useful interest prompts.

Change your position

Move from behind a lectern to centre stage; and in a smaller room, move from a flip chart to stand closer to one of the listeners. If you have been sitting, stand; and vice versa. In an informal setting, consider perching on the edge of a table in order to vary your position.

Use a visual aid

Be careful not to use a visual aid only as an interest prompt (see Chapters 5 and 6 on visual aids). Write on the flip chart, show a slide or pass round a sample.

Do something unexpected

Take off your shoe and bang it on the desk to make your point.

Ask a question

Involve the audience by asking one of the following kinds of questions:

1. Rhetorical – the listeners will be prompted to give a mental response, e.g. 'Where can we find the solution to this problem?'

2. General question answered by a show of hands: 'Who has installed a new computer system in the last year? Put up your hand.'

3. General question answered by one or two people with a direct answer: 'Who here can give me the details of a problem that they have encountered?'

4. Direct question: 'Mr Smith, what did you do when the fire destroyed all your records?'

Except for 1 above, always wait for an answer; remember the audience needs time to adjust from passive listening to active participation, so don't be afraid of the silence.

Involve the audience in action

• Ask them to work out a calculation, using their own situation as a base and applying the theory which you have just presented.

• Ask the small/medium audience to move to a demonstration table to see a model in action and, better still, get involved in some way.

• Ask for a volunteer to write on the flip chart.

• Ask them to turn to the person sitting next to them and discuss a point raised in your talk.

You'll see in Chapter 2 Preparing and Planning a Presentation that your talk should include several interest prompts at various points to add variety.

Other ways of preventing boredom

During the coffee breaks, if possible, open all windows to get a change of air, particularly if you have a smoky atmosphere. You could also ask people to stand and stretch.

I had to speak in the Graveyard Spot, i.e. after lunch, at a conference in a hotel venue, with no windows and to an audience of approximately 100 business people who had been sitting all the morning and had indulged in a good lunch. What a challenge! As I was addressing them on the importance of presentation skills, I decided to emphasise breathing and voice projection, and asked them to join me in several exercises. After a reluctant start, they all participated and no one had the opportunity of going to sleep.

I have seen the third speaker in a long evening's presentation ask the audience to stand and move about on the spot to get rid of 'dead bums' before she began her talk.

Formal business presentations with senior executives may not be the place to practise some of these techniques, but do be aware, that as the speaker, you are in control of the audience. If their concentration is lagging, your objectives will not be achieved and your talk will not be remembered.

SUMMARY

- Bear in mind that different-sized audiences behave differently.

- Research your audience.

- Watch their body language.

- Use comprehension questions in small groups.

- Control the interruptions.

- Use interest prompts.

18

Persuading, Selling and Convincing

'You can't learn anything while you are talking'
BING CROSBY (in BBC interview with Michael Parkinson 1975)

Interaction with the audience is a universally acceptable goal, but a good speaker is also a good seller. There are some people who think selling is a dirty word. For them, the very idea of a salesperson conjures up a picture of a pushy, fast-talking individual whose sole aim is to force his customers to buy against their will. Worst of all, he doesn't listen. Faced with such a hard sale, his customers may feel that their only option is to sign on the dotted line. Most of us have experienced such horrors at one time or another and they tend to colour our view of selling.

In this chapter I want to suggest some ways in which you can improve *your* selling techniques, because, whether you recognise it or not you're involved in selling every day of your life. You may wonder how I can make such a claim. Think back over the last few days to the decisions you have made in your working environment. Were all your ideas and views totally supported by everyone who was involved? I doubt it. I imagine that you had to coax, influence, cajole, urge, even insist and impel people to follow what you believed to be the right course of action. In that process you were selling your ideas and your opinions. I have linked persuading, convincing and selling together in one chapter heading because I believe they are all part of the same skill.

One reason why you may dislike the idea of selling is because, like telling a joke, it requires a positive reaction from the listener, and if the response is not forthcoming, you feel you are being rejected. This is in fact a misconception. It is your opinion or idea that is being rejected, not you. This is a hard lesson to learn. In my early days of selling, I often felt discouraged by a seemingly endless wall of 'No thank you, dear, not today'. Fortunately I was able to improve my techniques, so eventually I received more acceptances than rejections. In the commercial world the reason for your speaking will often be to persuade, convince and sell. I want to draw together some of the themes that run through this book and show how you can use them to achieve support and agreement for your views more easily.

Pitching For Clients

Business is based on the ability to win clients. Today, professional services such those provided by lawyers, accountants, management consultants, bankers and surveyors all have to learn how to pitch competitively for new business.

Although this chapter is not designed as a guide on pitching for business, many of the suggestions can be useful in gaining support and commitment.

Prepare to Persuade

Your first step to successful persuasion is researching your listeners. What are their concerns and what are their problems? What do you know about them? It is impossible to persuade if you don't know their present position. In an extreme case you might find that they already agree with you and need no convincing. Your listeners have views and opinions as well as difficulties and anxieties that will influence their acceptance or rejection of your ideas.

In Chapter 19 Meeting the Media, I refer to open questions that managers employ to gain full and comprehensive answers. Open questions generally start with who, what, when, why, where or how. Use them to discover more about your listeners' opinions. 'What do you think the effect will be if we agree to the overtime ban?' 'How can we achieve these results in less time?' Reverse roles with your listener and let him state his case as fully as possible, but remember also to ask for reasons why he supports a particular view. If you are managing a sales force, you may need to persuade your reps of the importance of completing paperwork. If you can discover their reason for disliking it, you will be halfway to overcoming their prejudice. Sometimes people are reluctant to express their doubts or fears about a course of action, because they feel that it will reflect on their ability to complete a task. I am often faced with managers who dislike admitting that they feel nervous when speaking in public. I try to persuade them that recognising their anxiety is the first step to handling it.

You may be attempting to convince a colleague to change her mind, but until you can uncover the reasons for her views, you won't be successful. Her views may be based on faulty information. 'All the operators arrive late in the morning and leave early at the end of the day.' She may have had previous experience, which she has misinterpreted or which has jaundiced her thinking. If you don't identify her viewpoint and the reasons for it, your sound and well-reasoned arguments will go sailing straight past her, because they are not correctly targeted. You must have the bull's-eye in your sights before you can hit it.

Developing Your Listening Skills

You may need to improve your listening skills before you can persuade successfully. In Chapter 1 What is Communication?, I gave reasons why listening isn't easy and I suggested some ways in which speakers could help to minimise the difficulties.

You can also help yourself to be a better listener. Remember that some of the major barriers to effective listening are internal. When, as a listener, you go down Route 350, you are allowing yourself to be distracted by your own thoughts. So concentrate and don't allow your own experience and prejudices to block out what you're hearing. Listen with an open mind to the content and disregard the distractions of irritating mannerisms and poor delivery. I find this a great challenge. Much of my working day is spent assessing and correcting speakers, so that it has become second nature. When I am 'off duty' and in a social situation, I have to silence my inner thoughts such as 'What a pity she doesn't open her mouth more when she speaks' or 'Why does he keep saying yes at the end of every sentence?' Don't fall into the trap of letting poor presentation prevent you from listening well.

Instead of going down Route 350, you can use your spare brain capacity to summarise mentally and to recap on what the speaker is telling you. This can be particularly useful if the speaker is presenting information in a jumbled and unstructured manner. As each idea is presented, you can mentally categorise it so that you'll be able to recall it at a later stage.

Don't forget your body language when you are listening. Your eye contact and facial expression should be encouraging. Show your interest by smiling, nodding, saying 'I see, I understand' and asking questions, 'So why was that?' Listening needs to be visual to the speaker.

Successful persuasion often depends upon your demonstrating an understanding of the listeners' viewpoint. Showing that you recognise their problem can help to build a rapport that increases your credibility. Don't be too quick to present your own ideas. Register that you have heard what they've told you by repeating their views. This is an indication that you have listened, not that you agree with them: 'So you're worried that if we extend the period of payment, we would have a cash flow problem?', 'So from your point of view, asking the secretaries to work overtime could lead to resentment?', 'I see, so you're telling me that if you installed new equipment as planned it could cause disruption at a very busy time of year?'

What Are the Needs of Your Listeners?

In Chapter 2 Preparing and Planning a Presentation, I mentioned satisfying some of the needs of management as well as those of the workforce. Everyone has their own particular need that they seek to satisfy, as well as problems they want to solve. So find out what your listeners want. Do they have a difficulty that needs resolving? What are they hoping to achieve? What are they aiming for? It may be as simple as an afternoon in which the telephone doesn't ring or as ambitious as doubling the previous year's profits.

I remember a management consultant telling me that when she talked to a new client, she always tried to identify 'the pain'. In other words, what was causing her client anxiety? Her client might identify 'the pain' like this: 'If only we could find staff who took an interest in their jobs . . .' or 'If only we could be sure of getting the spare parts on time . . .' Find out what is your listeners' 'if only'. What is their fantasy? Ask questions and listen to the answers.

Don't Interrupt

With inarticulate, long-winded speakers, it is very tempting to supply words that they are searching for or even to finish their sentences for them. Resist the temptation. It will be seen as an interruption. Don't jump in immediately the speaker has finished speaking, but allow a few seconds' silence. He will know from this that you have been listening and not simply waiting for your turn to speak. Most importantly, he will be ready to listen to you. He will feel that he doesn't have to battle with you for a chance to be heard. Therefore, your chances of persuading him are increased.

What Do They Know and What Do They Think of You?

Now that you understand your listeners' position, you need to discover how much they already know about your views. You may recall from Chapter 2 Preparing and Planning a Presentation that this level of knowledge can be multi-layered:

- What do they know?

- What do they think they know?

- What do they want to know?

- What do they need to know in order for you to convince and persuade them?

If your listeners have no background information and you intend to persuade them on a new course of action, you'll need to lay some foundation before you start. But, you'll quickly lose their attention if they feel that you are talking down to them. Don't underestimate the risks of miscalculating your listeners' level of understanding and knowledge.

Don't bore your colleagues in a meeting with historical facts that everyone knows. Don't do the reverse and assume that they already have enough information to understand your presentation. I remember vividly presenting a complex training programme to a board of directors, having already sent a written proposal to the training director. It was only later that

I realised the rest of the board had not seen the written proposal and therefore were unable to follow or understand most of my presentation.

You will also need to know what their attitude is towards you and your views: Are they in favour?, Are they indifferent? Or are they opposed? A listener who is well informed but who is opposed to you will require a different approach from one who is indifferent and uninformed.

More questions and more listening will supply the answers to help you plan your strategy for successful persuasion. To convince people, you need to appeal to their minds and to their emotions – one supports the other.

Information for Their Minds

Early on in your persuasion, establish why your audience should listen to you. Tell them what's in it for them. For example, 'By using our services we believe you could reduce your tax bill by 25 per cent' or 'I am going to show you various techniques you can use to overcome the backlog in the warehouse.' Remember, you shouldn't tell them that you are going to convince or persuade them that one or other of the techniques is superior. This is, of course, what you may hope to do during your presentation, but it must appear that the decision is left to your listeners.

Expand on what they already know and add new points. If their level of knowledge is minimal, you may decide to present your information in a series of talks, rather than at one session. There is a limit to the amount of new material that can be absorbed at any one time. As you present the reasons for your opinions, remember to identify the areas of mutual agreement: 'You will see that we both agree on . . .' In this manner you will demonstrate your acceptance of some of your listeners' views that will provide a favourable climate in which to discuss the more controversial points. Try to minimise your differences and discount your minor points of disagreement, so that you can concentrate on persuading them to accept your views on the larger issues.

Remember that you need to summarise constantly and to recap. Make sure that your persuasive talk also has an easy-to-follow structure and that your ideas are illustrated with relevant examples.

Persuasion at Meetings

Various estimates have been made about the total number of hours managers spend in meetings every year and assessments have also been made on the total cost of these meetings. In your next idle moment, maybe at an unproductive meeting, look around the room and calculate how much it is costing the company, in salaries alone, to have those people sitting at the table. The real cost is probably two or three times that sum. You can see how the company benefits and the managers save time by reducing the amount of time spent at inefficient meetings.

How to chair a meeting

Many of the skills you will need for chairing a meeting or leading a discussion are already referred to in earlier chapters. Your planning and preparation for a meeting should fall under the same three headings:

- setting an objective;

- researching your audience;

- designing a structure.

Setting an objective

Many meetings are held for the wrong reasons. Groups may follow traditional patterns of behaviour – 'We always have a meeting on Thursdays' – and it is often necessary to question the real purpose. Some of the more common reasons are:

• selling ideas and products;

• solving problems;

• giving and getting information;

• taking decisions.

If you are responsible for the meeting you must be clear why the meeting is taking place and what you hope it will achieve. Make sure that a memo or a couple of phone calls couldn't accomplish as much, but in less time.

Researching your audience

All the questions you asked in preparation for being persuasive are relevant here. You should try and limit the number of people attending the meeting. An ideal number is between six and seven. Meetings where more than ten are present either include silent observers or, if everyone contributes, become unmanageable. Divide up larger groups so that your meeting is more productive. Make sure everyone is aware of the purpose of the meeting and of their role in it. Don't invite anyone to the meeting who is not essential for achieving your objective. 'Assistants' who accompany their bosses are usually superfluous – you probably need one or the other but not both.

Designing a structure

Your preparation must include a detailed agenda that is circulated well in advance of the meeting so that everyone has a chance to prepare. Decide whether to schedule items in order of importance or of length. Beware of short, unimportant items, like deciding the new position of the noticeboard, which can develop into a half-hour discussion. You can often assess the likely time needed for a particular item by talking to the people concerned. If they appear to be in total disagreement you may decide to have a pre-meeting to sort out some of their differences. This will make more efficient use of the time scheduled for the main meeting.

The structure of a problem-solving meeting could be designed like this:

- describe the problem;

- discuss the background and reasons for it;

- brain-storm solutions;

- evaluate solutions;

- give recommendations.

You should aim to focus on finding solutions rather than on attributing blame. By concentrating on finding answers, the meeting will have a more positive attitude and be more active.

Opening statements

As chairperson, your introduction sets the scene for the meeting and should stimulate interest in all the items scheduled for discussion. Try to inject a sense of urgency into the meeting so that everyone contributes. Be sure to announce the reason for the meeting and what you hope to accomplish. Also, include some benefits for the participants: 'I want to finalise the budget for next year at this meeting. That means you will be able to plan your staffing requirements immediately and begin the year with a full production team.' Ensure that the timescale is understood, so that long, open-ended discussions are avoided.

Introduction

Give the background to the first item and open the discussion with a directed question: 'George, you're the one at the sharp end facing customers, can you tell us what caused this latest crisis?' You could also use a general question: 'So that's the situation at present. How do the rest of you think we should tackle it?'

How to control the meeting

The most powerful method of keeping control of your group is by *asking questions* and *recapping and summarising*. I have given examples of two styles of questions (directed and general) in the section above and you can also use the following.

Redirected questions

You ask another member of the group to answer a question that has been directed to you. For example, George has stated that he will need more envelopes to complete the mailing and asks if you have any in stock. You reply, 'Mary I think this is one for you. When will we receive the new shipment of envelopes?'

Relay question

You relay the question back to the group. 'Before I answer that let me ask *you*. Where do *you* think we should have the Christmas party?'

Reverse question

You encourage the questioner to answer his or her own question. 'What do you think? Are people prepared to pay an extra £20 for a faster service?'

Summaries

Regular summaries will help people concentrate on the main points and avoid interesting but irrelevant side issues. You will remember that in your talk you included interest prompts and rhetorical questions to gather up the stragglers who had wandered off down Route 350. Summarising during a meeting serves a similar purpose. There are two types:

- interim summaries;
- final summary.

Interim summaries

You can report progress in the course of the discussion and help to refocus everyone's attention: 'Maybe we could leave the question of what happened at last year's Christmas party and try to decide where we want to have it this year. So far we've considered the Manor House which is reasonably priced but difficult to get to and the new place in the High Street which is central but we don't know if it's any good.'

With an interim summary you can also tie up one point and move on to the next: 'So we are agreed that there has been an increase in absenteeism in all the departments. The next step we need to consider is what we can do about it.'

Use interim summaries to highlight important points: 'We've covered the cost of the relocation, and the loss of production while the factory is closed. We have also looked at the disruptive factor for our staff. Those are the main points so far.'

Don't forget the value of visually displaying the main conclusion of the meeting. Use a flip chart to write up each point as it is covered. This is visual proof that you are achieving your objectives and an encouragement to the group when the discussion appears to have become bogged down.

An important effect of summarising regularly is that it enables the minute-taker to check whether or not they have recorded the principal elements.

Final summary

Your final summing up should give a sense of achievement to the group. When a discussion has been heated, it's particularly important to draw together the various factions and unite them in a common course of action. As well as agreement from everyone, you need to establish commitment. Make sure that everyone present knows what they are responsible for and the timescale in which it must be accomplished.

SUMMARY

- Understand your listeners' needs.
- Involve your listeners.
- Use persuasion at meetings.
- Control the discussion.
- Get commitment.

19

Meeting the Media

'No question is so difficult to answer as that to
which the answer is obvious'
GEORGE BERNARD SHAW

Many of the skills you have learnt in order to speak more effectively within your working environment, together with your
skills of persuasion, selling and conviction also apply to press
interviews, and in this chapter I am going to show how you can
benefit from any interaction with the media.

You may think that this chapter isn't relevant to you, as you'll
never have to appear on radio or TV or even be interviewed by a
newspaper journalist, but consider the value of personal publicity as well as the publicity for your company and its products
that is offered by any media exposure. It is free advertising: 'The
business that believes that advertising is not necessary may find
that customers take the same attitude about their business'
(Anon). In fact, press coverage is better than advertising.
Anyone looking at an advertisement knows that it is designed
and paid for by the manufacturer of the product and therefore
can only present a very subjective view. Your name in print or
your face on TV has much more impact as you haven't bought
the space. Presenting a positive image of your company in a

media interview is invaluable and consequently public relations companies spend much time attempting to obtain exposure in the press for their clients and their products.

Your immediate reaction to a press approach may be to say 'no comment' or to refer the enquirer to your company's public relations department. You may not trust the press because they seem to manipulate the truth and fail to represent accurately the views of those to whom they speak. This is a universally held view; in a recent poll journalists were rated low in integrity and honesty – in fact at about the same level as politicians! Although this is a common view of the press, it is also incorrect as far as quality papers and the broadcasting media are concerned, and for you to benefit from media contact, you must understand how the media work.

What's the Angle?

Every story must have what is known as an 'angle'. This is the news hook or reason for its existence. When I was a radio journalist I often presented ideas for interviews or programmes to my producer who would immediately ask me, 'Why is this a good story? What is the point of doing it? Who is interested?' Or, more succinctly, he might say, 'So what? Who cares?' These are the questions which you must ask yourself, whether you are initiating a contact with the press or responding to an approach from them. A dull, rather humdrum subject can be of interest to the press provided you can identify a good angle. When I was seeking personal publicity a few years ago, I contacted a number of magazines prior to a business trip to Japan and told them that as a businesswoman in Japan, I was interested to discover whether I would be offered the male equivalent of a geisha girl. When I returned, I was interviewed by three different journalists on the problems and delights of travelling as a Western businesswoman in Japan. (No, there aren't any male equivalents to geisha girls.)

The journalists' staple diet is 'News' and yet it is an indefinable term. Ask ten press people to describe what constitutes 'News' and you will receive as many different answers. However, for the purposes of this book, I will exclude the possibility of you having to be interviewed on a major news item such as an air crash, a murder or your adulterous affair with a Hollywood star.

Coping With an Approach From the Press

You may well be flattered as well as a little apprehensive when you find a journalist wants to talk to you, so here are some guidelines to help you cope.

Saying no

You can refuse to speak to the press, but be sure you understand the consequences if you choose that course of action. The journalist's first contact will be by phone and when he has described why he has approached you, ask for time to think about his proposal, but do return his phone call promptly as he will have deadlines to meet. On some occasions, if you decide not to meet the press, you can suggest an alternative person to represent your company or association. However, if your views are personal and you decline to be interviewed, you can offer to be quoted 'off the record'. This will enable the journalist to include your comments and maintain a balance in his story. For example, on the radio you will hear a reporter saying, 'I have spoken to several managers within the industry and the consensus is that the strike will be over by the end of the week.' Or 'Sources close to the strike action committee claim that the latest pay offer will be turned down.' TV is mostly visual and 'unattributable sources', i.e. when the interviewer doesn't name his source, are quoted less frequently. On balance, I advise clients to co-operate with the press whenever possible, because your 'No comment' can easily be turned into 'He refused to speak to the press' with the implication that you have something to hide.

If you have a good excuse for not wanting to speak to the press, i.e. you don't have all the facts, or you are waiting for a report, tell the journalist your reason. Always refuse to comment on statements or quotations from articles by a third party until you have seen the full text. It is possible to transmit data rapidly across the country or even around the world, so you can justifiably insist that you must read the entire quote in context before responding.

Before you say yes

When you find you have a journalist on the telephone, don't be rushed into agreeing to take part in a programme or to be interviewed until you have a clear idea of what the angle is. In other words, why is the subject being covered? What makes it newsworthy? Why do they want you to contribute? Take control of the situation and of your tongue and reverse roles with the caller. Now is the time for you to interview the journalist and write down everything she says in answer to your questions. Her willingness or reluctance at this stage to discuss openly the reason for and the content of her article or programme will be a good indicator of her integrity. If necessary, ask her to slow down or repeat information until you are satisfied that you have enough data on which to base your decision to accept or decline her invitation. Find out her name, the name of her paper, or station and programme and when and where the interview will take place (if you are going to be on a business trip in Australia on the day in question, you don't need to continue your conversation).

Here is a check list of questions to ask before you agree to be interviewed:

- Why is the article being written or the programme being made?

- Why is the subject newsworthy?

- What is the angle?

- Why have you been approached?

- Who else's views are being sought?

- Who else will appear on the programme?

- Will it be broadcast live or will it be recorded?

If you are agreeable in principle, say so to the journalist at this point and tell her you will confirm later in the day or week. This allows you time to ponder on the most important question – what's in it for you? By gaining time, you may be able to watch or listen to the programme, or read the newspaper or journal if it is not familiar to you. You will also have the opportunity to seek the views of people within your company as to whether you should agree to be interviewed and to decide how the company would benefit. Here is a check list of questions for you to answer before you say yes:

- What's in it for me?

- What's in it for my company?

- Am I the best person to be interviewed?

- Do I want to be seen to associate with the other speakers or interviewees?

- Do I have sufficient time to prepare?

- Does the newspaper or journal have a good reputation?

- Do I trust the journalist?

- What will happen if I decline the invitation?

How to Approach the Media

This is not a book about press or public relations, so I shall only mention a few points to bear in mind if you are initiating contact with the press.

Earlier I said that the press lives on News – a term that's hard to define. However, if your contact with the media is to succeed, your story should be original and unusual, and should concern or affect sufficient people. Choosing the correct outlet for your story is important, i.e. a new development in concrete mixers won't interest the national press, but it may be a front-page story for *Builders Weekly*. Identify the news angle of your story, i.e. 500th employee has joined the company; you have received a design award for a new product; a senior executive has returned from a market expansion trip into China. Once you have a news hook, you must choose the correct outlet for it, i.e. your local newspaper or radio station may be interested in the 500th employee, particularly if you are located in an area of high unemployment; the *Design Gazette* or local TV may be interested in the design award; and *Exporting Today* or the Central Office of Information may be interested in the China trip. If you are unsure which journals or newspapers are suitable for your story, consult the directories of media listed at the back of this book (see page 292), also study the *Radio* and *TV Times* and listen to local radio stations.

Your initial approach to both print and broadcast media can be in the form of a press release, giving the gist of your story plus a contact name and number. Remember that during a telephone conversation with the broadcast media, they will be assessing *how* you're presenting yourself as well as the interest level of your story. Enthusiasm, vitality and sincerity are qualities that producers are always looking for.

Try to establish a continuing relationship with both your local papers and radio stations, and don't be discouraged if they don't accept your first approach, which may be due to factors outside your control, i.e. lack of time or space. Local

TV provides limited exposure, but it is a good learning ground should you ever need to appear on national TV.

After You Have Said Yes

Preparation is the key to successful interaction with the media and planning what you want to say and what you don't want to say is the first step. Remember, you only have one chance to get it right and no one will be interested in your second thoughts.

In the same way as you drew a mind map to release all your thoughts before you wrote a word of your talk, you can do the same for your media meeting. Remember to put down all the material you don't want to reveal, as well as that which you do. Code your ideas with three colours, say red for positive ideas to include, blue for points to exclude and yellow for ideas that don't fall into either category. Your red ideas will become the kernel of your interview and from them you should develop your key statements.

Target audience

In order to prepare well, you must find out as much as possible about your audience. Who reads the newspaper? Who watches or listens to the programme? Talking to the *Financial Times* or the *Finchley Times* requires a different approach; talking to a reporter from a BBC radio news desk or from *Woman's Hour* and being interviewed by a journalist from *Newsround* (a children's news programme) or from *Newsnight* are very different situations. Find out the age, sex, education and, most important, the socio-economic group of the target audience, so you can avoid talking down to the audience or losing their interest because they don't understand you.

Now is the time to familiarise yourself with the programme.

Record or video it so that you can study the style and techniques used by the presenters. Is there a bias? Is there evidence of heavy editing? Read articles in the newspaper or journal and analyse how the interviews are handled. Is the story balanced? If possible, contact any other people who are to be interviewed on the same subject and arrange to speak to them beforehand. If you need more information about the programme or article contact the journalist involved. Find out some of the questions she intends to ask (she won't divulge all of them), so that you can research any additional data you might need. Put yourself in her place and that of the editor or producer and ask yourself what questions they might pose. Too often my clients find it hard to accept that difficult questions should be anticipated and the correct answers carefully worked out. Hoping against hope that the journalist won't find the skeleton in your cupboard is foolhardy. Far better to put a smart suit on your skeleton so if the cupboards do open for a moment, it won't be recognised for what it is. Plan how you can turn your negative points into positive points.

Key statements

You will have decided to be interviewed because you recognised the benefit to you or your company or both, and now you must identify how you want your audience to react. Remember, the journalist is not your audience. Your audience is made up of the listeners, viewers or readers. Depending on the duration of the interview, choose one or two key statements that will form the core of your answers. Don't attempt to make more than three points. Don't add too much – most successful replies are 20–30 seconds only. Learn to talk in brief, colourful sentences. Find illustrations and anecdotes that will capture the imagination of your audience. Remember to avoid jargon and abbreviations that won't be understood by the general public. When dealing with the print media, you can afford to amplify your answers, but bear in mind that whatever you say will be condensed, rearranged and even cut by sub-editors after the journalist has written it.

Thorough preparation will enable you to put across your key statements concisely, colourfully and entertainingly, and will reduce the possibility of misrepresentation.

Steps in your preparation:

- research the target audience;

- identify your key statements, i.e. what you want to say and what you don't want to say;

- find colourful examples and anecdotes to illustrate your points.

At the Radio Station

The most important factor is your voice and your ability to project *enthusiasm*, *sincerity* and *vitality*.

Radio is an informal medium and you should try to concentrate on talking to the interviewer and forget the thousands or even millions who are listening to you at home. Research shows that most radio is listened to by people on their own and there is no group identity such as you'll find in a large conference hall or in a theatre. You are not addressing a group of thousands, you are talking to a number of individuals listening to you by themselves. Your words should be simple and they should paint pictures that will stir the listeners' imaginations. Try to illustrate your key statements with colourful examples.

I heard a story on the radio recently that illustrates what I mean. It was concerning the bad behaviour of drunken passengers on holiday charter planes. A stewardess was interviewed about an occasion when a plane had to make an unscheduled landing because a passenger had become uncontrollable and was attempting to open the emergency door. In answer to a question about how the stewardess felt about these unruly passengers she said, 'It is very, very upsetting for the younger girls who have never experienced such abuse. They look forward to doing this job and when they get on the plane they find it's worse than *being a barmaid in a rough pub*.' I think in a few words she painted a very clear picture.

Don't be overawed by the studio equipment or by the interviewer. You may well be in a small overheated studio with a glass wall through which the producer and technician will be sitting. Ignore the microphone and speak in a normal voice – a technician will adjust the levels. Always ask to see the introduction to your appearance in order to check for inaccuracies. Also ask what the first question will be, so that you are prepared.

Speak in a steady, conversational tone and avoid filler words ('You know', 'I mean') and refrain from beginning every answer with 'Well . . .' Don't use an impersonal style – 'People think that . . .' Instead say, 'I think that . . .' Being long-winded and rambling is a major sin. Give brief answers that don't run over 30 seconds and pause at the end of each one to enable the interviewer to ask another question. Radio interviews are generally 2–3 minutes in length, so you only have a short time in which to deliver your message. Avoid yes/no answers and aim to put a smile in your voice. The section on Question Time below should help you deal with the interview.

Find out, before you begin, how long the interview will be so that you can pace your answers accordingly. Never speak over someone else, even to add your agreement – 'Mm that's right' – but raise your voice if someone is interrupting you and say 'May I finish . . .' If the interview is recorded and you are dissatisfied with the quality of one of your answers, ask to re-record it.

If you have a tendency to fiddle, remove any temptations such as spectacles, earrings, bracelets, paper and pens. If you need a crib, write it on a card. Nerves can make you breathless, so take a couple of deep, relaxing breaths before you begin and try not to hold your breath during the interview. If the programme is recorded, make sure you know when it is scheduled for broadcast.

Television Appearances

The most memorable part of being on TV is your own appearance. Your credibility depends almost entirely on how you look, as viewers are convinced that they can instantly assess anyone within a few seconds of his appearing in their screen. In the 1990s, several politicians found to their cost that in spite of being proficient and experienced, they lost the support of the voters because their faces or personalities weren't popular on TV. It is unlikely that your career depends on TV success, but be aware that it is a very powerful medium.

Rehearse your body language

TV is very intimate. The TV camera comes closer than most of your friends. Few people look at you from a distance of only a few inches and yet a close-up on TV from your chin to your hairline reveals much of your inner feelings and thoughts. You need to build up your confidence so your uncertainty doesn't show. Remember, familiarity breeds confidence, so the more you can learn about TV before you appear, the more confident you will be. Watch the programme and notice the seating arrangements and the colour of the set; study the camera angles and become aware of the cutting from one camera to another to pick up interest points; familiarise yourself with the style of interview and the types of questions that are posed.

During your practice sessions at home, try sitting in a chair similar to that which you will find in the TV studio, and avoid crossing and recrossing your legs or swinging your foot. Don't fiddle with the arm of the chair – arrange your hands calmly in your lap. Sit well back into the seat of the chair and don't slouch. While you are rehearsing in your seated position, try to put animation, enthusiasm and enjoyment into your face, but keep your head still as the camera can't keep following it if it's jerking about. If you study TV interviews and panel discussions, you'll see that most of the camera shots are of head and shoulders, so all your expression must be in your face.

Smile appropriately and maintain a confident and enthusiastic appearance, but be sure to match your look with the content of the interview. One politician I counselled had the unfortunate habit of smiling broadly when he discussed the problem of unemployment and was unaware of the impression he created until I recorded him on video.

The point made in Chapter 10 How to Look Confident about using your hands is doubly important on TV. Keep your hands away from your face, don't touch your hair, nose, mouth and don't fiddle with pens, jewellery or your clothing. Your hands should be still and not straightening your tie or rearranging your necklace.

Never look at the camera – in fact, try to imagine that no one else is in the studio apart from the interviewer. When you are being introduced, look at her with interest and avoid a smug or an embarrassed grin as she lists your qualities and achievements. During questions, as well as when you are answering, keep your eyes on her and remember that the camera will often pick up your reaction to a question, so don't grimace or pull a face. In a discussion programme, look at the speaker and try to appear interested and alert; act naturally and nod or shake your head in agreement or disagreement. Remember to keep your head up because if the lighting is poor, you will appear to have heavy shadows under your eyes.

It may help you to control your nervousness to remember that the average audience for one TV set is two to three individuals, so imagine having a conversation with friends in your own sitting room and try to forget the millions who may be watching you.

What to wear on TV

Try to avoid wearing black or dark grey or even mid-blue, which comes out very dark on camera, as these colours can look too sombre, even for a business programme. Grey is most suitable for men, but avoid white shirts and choose beige or pale blue instead. Don't wear material with any narrow stripes or checks and avoid red as it can 'bleed'. Also, avoid large patterns; plain colours look best on camera. Avoid jangling earrings and fussy necklines, and remember that most of the camera shots will be head and shoulders so that you should aim for a simple, plain, uncluttered look. Shiny jewellery is a distraction as it catches the light. If possible, check the colour of the background set before the programme so that you don't choose an outfit that clashes, or tones in so well that you disappear.

At the TV station

Adrenaline and alcohol don't mix so refuse a drink to calm your nerves as it may have the opposite effect. Take a deep breath instead or a small soft drink and remember to go to the toilet before and after your make-up session.

Make-up session

As the lights are very hot, you will certainly perspire and give the impression you are under pressure and feeling uneasy. That's probably exactly how you will be feeling, but why tell millions of people? A quick pat with the powder puff will enable you to look composed. If you are fair, the lights will bleach out your colouring so expect to have your eyes made up. Allow 10 minutes for the make-up session, which will be conducted by make-up experts who are also trained to calm and relax you before your appearance. If you suffer from any allergies, take your own make-up.

In the studio

When you see the studio set for the first time, you will be surprised that it looks rather tacky and smaller than it appears on your TV at home. The person in charge in the studio is the floor manager who is in contact with the director in the production control room, which is generally positioned above the studio behind a large glass wall. In the studio, there may be an assistant floor manager. Take the opportunity of visiting the studio before your appearance if you can, to familiarise yourself with the set-up; this will help you concentrate on the interview when it's your turn so that you can avoid being distracted while on camera.

Now it's your turn

A technician will clip on a personal mike to your shirt or jacket; it's advisable for women to wear a button-through shirt or dress as high necks without a front fastening have no suitable place to which the mike can be fixed. You should also avoid wearing silk, as this can cause crackling on the mike. Table-top and boom microphones are sometimes used as back-up and you can ignore them altogether.

When you are in position on the set, glance at the monitors on the floor in front of you to inspect your position on camera. Now is the time to straighten your tie, pull down your jacket and undo a button if necessary, or smooth your skirt and check your hair. This is not vanity – you don't want your credibility to be jeopardised by a stray wisp of hair or a crooked tie. Don't perch on the edge of the chair; sit well back so that you can easily move forward or backwards. Try to maintain an open position towards the camera and when you make a gesture use the arm furthest from the camera.

Check your introduction with the interviewer if you have not done so already; inaccuracies and even the mispronunciation of your name in the first few seconds of the interview are not a good start. Also confirm the duration of the piece. If you are feeling tension around your mouth and eyes, do some exercises to release the stiffness, and raise and lower your shoulders to become more relaxed (see Chapter 9 Relaxation Exercises). Several deep breaths will have a calming influence. Try to ignore your thumping heart and the rest of the studio, and imagine that you are about to have a private conversation with the interviewer.

The floor manager counts down from ten to zero and the interviewer faces the camera with her introduction. From now until the end of the programme, remember that the camera may be on you at any point, even when you are not talking. When the interview is over, don't thank the interviewer and *don't move.* Stay where you are until you are told you can get up. Even though sound and lights may have faded, the cameras will probably still be on the set, so don't leap up and shout in relief that it's all over!

Question Time

Reading a newspaper article doesn't give you much insight into the questioning techniques of the journalist, but by watching and listening to television and radio interviews you can learn more about the types of question that are often used.

Open questions

As part of their everyday work, managers tend to use open questions to gain as much information as possible about a situation or a subject to help them in the decision-making process: 'So what will be the outcome if we change from cardboard to plastic containers?', 'How can we cope with the new pay demands?', 'Why did you leave your last job?' Open questions are generally prefaced with what, why, when, how, where and who. Both media and print journalists use them when they want ample and full answers to their questions. The purpose of the interview is to hear the interviewee's views and opinions, and therefore it's the journalist's job to make sure her questions prompt interesting answers.

All the media are there to inform and to entertain, and the ratio of information to entertainment varies from one programme (or newspaper) to another. The BBC's *Nine O'Clock News* presents a high proportion of information, but with sufficient entertainment to ensure that the viewer keeps tuned. On the other hand, a games show will have a higher degree of entertainment and less information. In any newsagents, you will notice the differing amounts of hard news or lightweight stories that dominate the front pages of the national daily newspapers. The reason I am emphasising the element of entertainment present in all media is because the journalist is aware that information alone can be dull. It is in the journalist's interest, therefore, to stimulate and provoke exciting answers from you.

Statement questions

These questions can be answered by a yes or a no response and are generally avoided by good broadcast journalists. To illustrate this point, here is an extract from an interview with the oldest man in Birmingham recorded by a local radio journalist, in which the journalist lost control by asking the wrong kind of question.

'I expect you're very excited to be 98 years old?'
'No.'
'Well, I expect your family is very excited?'
'No.'
'I know that many people are very proud of you. Are you going to have a big party?'

'No.'
'Ninety-eight years is a grand old age and there have been
many changes in Birmingham since you were born. Have
you noticed a lot of changes in 98 years?'
'Not really.'
'You seem very healthy for your age. What's the secret of
your old age?'
'Dunno!' (He might have answered, not wasting his breath
answering silly questions.)

As you can see, this doesn't make for very exciting listening.
However, statement questions in the hands of a skilled *print*
journalist can become a good story:

'Were you expecting such a sharp fall in the share price?'
'No!'
'I expect it came as a bit of a shock then?'
'Yes, it did!'
'What about the future? Could the price go lower?'
'Well, yes.'

This could be written as follows: 'Gold-Top Chairman, Peter
Davis, is shocked by the fall in the share price, and he predicts
that there is worse to come.'

How to Make Key Statements

Don't try to avoid answering the question. You have probably
seen and heard politicians side-step questions and at home you
find yourself saying in frustration, 'Answer the question.'
Journalists are very adept at repeating and rephrasing questions, so you are ill-advised to evade them. Answer the question
and, without pausing for breath, say 'But the point I should
like to emphasise is that we have had fewer accidents in our
factory than any other company in this area.' This is your key

statement. You can also use phrases like 'But let me put it another way . . .', followed by your key statement, or 'But what I think is really important is . . .', followed by your key statement, or 'But what you shouldn't forget is . . .', followed by your key statement.

Don't feel restricted by the questions but control the interview by adding your key statement. Remember to include anecdotes: 'I can best answer that question by telling you about an incident that happened in our Manchester office.'

If you are unlucky enough to be interviewed by an inexperienced journalist, you may find that he answers his own questions: 'How do you feel about winning the contract? I expect you're very pleased. Everyone at your company must be very proud, as I know the competition was very great. It certainly is a great honour.' Try not to get drawn into this verbose nonsense and ignore his prompts. 'My company, Greystone Limited, was chosen to design and build a series of hotels in Florida and California. We think it's particularly significant that an English company and one from this area was awarded the contract, as the competition from American companies was very stiff. We feel it proves that Greystone Limited represented the best in British architecture.' Don't be self-conscious about naming your product or service, as this was one of the reasons for agreeing to a media meeting and you must not lose sight of it. You may be looking at the interviewer, but you are really talking to the audience listening to you at home or who will read your comments in the newspaper.

Don't wait for the right question

It may appear from this that you will never win with a journalist because he will always be in control of the questions. But remember that you are in control of the answers. You have decided what you want to say and you must say it without waiting for the right question. The right question may never come or it may come at the end of a long interview and your answer may be edited out.

In the face of hostile questioning

Everyone approached by the press is concerned that they will have to defend themselves against a barrage of aggressive and abrasive questions.

Be sure you understand the difference between hard questions and hostile questions. It's the journalist's job to make an interesting programme or write an interesting article, and a cosy chat, although more comfortable for you, is dull for everyone else. The journalist represents the voice of the people, so expect him to pose the questions they would ask if put face to face with you. A reporter will often play devil's advocate to provoke a more exciting answer from you. This is an example of a bland question: 'Following your appointment as Chairman, could you describe your plans for the future of the Company?' A better, and therefore tougher, question, is 'How did you formulate the new plans for the company' or 'How do you defend your new plans for the future of the Company to those who say that they're not achievable?'

You shouldn't treat this as a confrontation and respond in an antagonistic manner. Never lose your cool. Simply stand your ground and defend your point of view in a reasonable tone, with facts and not emotion. If you feel you are being asked a leading question, hold up your hand and dispute it. Don't let the interviewer get away with inaccuracies or distortions of the truth.

If the journalist discovers your weak point, you should admit it immediately. This may well disconcert him, if he was expecting you to disagree, and it will allow you enough time during the rest of the interview to put over some positive points: 'Yes, it is true that some of our kitchens were found to be unhygienic and had to be closed, but the point I'd like to emphasise is that we have taken the opportunity to install new equipment and have decorated throughout. Everyone will be delighted that our restaurants will be reopened in time for the Christmas parties.' Don't attempt to evade questions as journalists have a highly developed sense of smell for a good story and they will keep after you, but be prepared to turn negative points into positive statements with good explanations for apparent weaknesses.

Beware of hearing more in a question than the interviewer intends. You may well have a skeleton in the cupboard that you are worried will be dragged out for all the world to see; you may even have taken the precaution of preparing some suitable answers, but listen carefully to the question. Don't fall into the trap of answering a simple question with a detailed, defensive response. Parents are often concerned with how well they will answer their children's questions about the facts of life and so the question 'Mummy, where did I come *from*?' is answered with a half-hour detailed biology lesson. The parent might be rather nonplussed when the child says, 'Thanks, Mummy, I wanted to know 'cos Mary comes from Wales.'

Sometimes you need to reveal your hand slowly, point by point. One simple piece of information may be enough to satisfy the interviewer and if not, you still have some extra material up your sleeve. Because you have planned how you will handle problematic areas, there is no need to give the equivalent of a full-scale biology lesson immediately you hear the difficult question.

Summing up with a slant

Media journalists who are anxious to leave the listener or viewer with a particular opinion will sometimes fail to summarise accurately. If you feel that you are being misrepresented, correct the interviewer immediately in a reasonable voice. Your sincerity and honesty will make a good, lasting impression.

Off the record

Before the interview starts, you may tell the journalist that there is an area you can't answer questions about. However, if during the course of the meeting he refers to it, how should you respond? Quite simply you should remind him of your agreement: 'We did agree that you wouldn't ask questions about that because of the security aspect but I am happy to talk about the rest of the project.' Interviewers will often attempt to get you to say more than you intend, but remain calm and reasonable and refuse to answer, being sure to give the reason so that you don't appear to be concealing information. If you appear honest, sincere and straightforward you will gain credibility.

Don't repeat an interviewer's allegations in your denials: the interviewer might say, 'It appears that the company is in difficulties and close to bankruptcy.' Your reply should contain positive statements: 'That is not so. In fact, the company is on a sound financial footing and has the full backing of the shareholders.' This is a more powerful statement than 'The company is not close to bankruptcy.'

Discussions

You'll find that the objective of a broadcast discussion is often to present a number of different points of view without necessarily reaching a specific conclusion. The choice may be left to the listener or viewer. Remember, there will be competition for air time during the discussion and you will need to feel assertive in order to make your points.

Before you agree to take part, find out who else is on the

programme and what viewpoints they represent. The producers may seek to present a stimulating programme by having a contrast of opinions so you shouldn't expect to find fellow souls on the panel.

In order to present your opinions forcefully, you must have sufficient data to support them and to counteract arguments from your opponents. Also, remember to research into their backgrounds for further ammunition.

Discussions are often pre-recorded so that the dull patches can be edited, resulting in a more enjoyable and entertaining programme. Make sure you speak in headlines and don't ramble. Listen attentively to distinguish between evidence, argument and conclusions; examine the evidence offered by the other speakers to see if it is relevant or consistent; look at the assumptions underlying their conclusions to see if they are logical and, lastly, add a touch of humour to persuade your audience.

Telephone Interviews

Print interviews are often conducted over the phone. However, if the journalist is unknown to you, try to persuade him to talk to you face to face. In this way, you are in more control of the situation and can judge how much it is advisable to say. Radio interviews are sometimes conducted over the phone when the story is hot news, but before you begin you should establish the parameters of the interview as well as the time limit. Talk in short, punchy sentences and in a normal tone of voice.

Unless you find yourself at the centre of a major news story in an inaccessible part of the world, you are unlikely to be interviewed over the phone for TV. However, interviews are occasionally conducted in a regional studio by a national interviewer in, say, London. Respond to the interviewer as if he were in the room with you and try to look animated and lively as the camera records your responses. On this occasion you do look at the camera.

Interviews in the Office

If you are fortunate enough to be offered an interview in your office, accept it. You will feel more confident when you are on home ground and it is less time-consuming for you. Make sure that the background area looks tidy and that your telephone is unplugged. Radio interviews are often conducted in offices or hotel rooms with little disruption to the normal routine, except to ban telephone calls and to switch off background noise such as air conditioning or heating. TV recordings are more disruptive, as additional people and equipment are involved, and they may need to move your furniture in order to provide a suitable background. Make sure that constant cups of tea and coffee are available and you will be popular with everyone.

Press Conferences

These are called to respond to bad news or to announce good news.

If a negative story breaks about your company or organisation, you may want to call a press conference to refute the story or to present your own angle. Think carefully of the benefit of this because you may be in danger of prolonging a small, one-day story into a larger two-day or three-day exposure. If a press conference seems the correct path, open with a brief statement that conveys your company's objective. This press statement should also be in a written form, so that it can be handed out to journalists. You may choose to have two or three spokespeople present to answer questions, but ensure that a time limit is imposed from the beginning.

Good news is more fun for you but less newsworthy and so,

to attract a good attendance, you must make it a special occasion. There is considerable competition for journalists' time so plan an original incentive to draw them. The services of a good public relations company are always beneficial in all your interactions with the press, and if you find you are appearing more frequently, consider a short course in media training to build your confidence and add polish to your performance.

A Last Word

Remember to treat all journalists with respect, but not reverence or familiarity. You are the expert so listen to the question, answer it concisely and include your key statements, but challenge any misleading information.

SUMMARY

- Discover the reason for the invitation.

- What's in it for you?

- Prepare thoroughly.

- Watch or listen to the programme. Read the newspaper.

- Rehearse, rehearse and rehearse.

- Remain cool, calm and confident – you are the expert.

20

Virtual and Cross-cultural Meetings

'I know that you believe you understand what you think I said, but I am not sure that you realise that what you heard is not what I meant'

ANON

Apart from handling TV, radio or the press you may find yourself giving your presentation using modern technology to reach an audience around the world or addressing people from different cultural backgrounds. In this chapter I will examine the advantages and disadvantages of using technology to communicate and offer some suggestions on how to get the most from it; I am also going to give a brief overview of the problems you may face with cross-cultural meetings and, lastly, give some recommendations for using interpreters.

Virtual Meetings

Virtual meetings using audio-, data- or video-conferencing technology have increased substantially over the past few years. They represent not only significant savings in time and money, but also reduce the stress levels of managers who previously had to spend many days travelling and nights away from home.

However, there are situations and cultures where physical face-to-face communication cannot be replaced by technology. Initial meetings, where the foundation for a good working relationship is built, need to be real and not virtual. In fact, if a social element such as a meal can be introduced, this will speed up the process.

In cultures such as the Middle East and the Far East, business is conducted with a personal relationship focus, whereas in northern Europe and the US the focus is on striking the deal. I was unaware of this difference when I met a client from an Arab country a few years ago. I got down to business straight away, in order not to waste the time of this VIP. Later I learnt that this approach was considered impolite and I should have spent time on the non-business topics before indirectly raising the reason for our meeting.

In countries where the approach to time is less than precise virtual meetings may also be inappropriate. Those in the Mediterranean countries and Latin America have a 'fluid' attitude to time and regard North Americans as being too inflexible. While working in the Middle East my colleagues and I were often frustrated as our client's clock seemed to run an hour behind ours.

With the virtual technologies there is a reduction in the usual channels of communication: that the lack of a non-verbal expression such as a raised eyebrow or the speaker leaning forward can affect how his message comes across during an audio conference; eye contact during a video conference may be directed towards the listeners but it will lack the impact of a speaker in the same room. Obviously nothing can replace the value of real meetings for contentious or sensitive issues where minor nuances of body language can often say more than words.

However, even with these limitations, there is no doubt that technology plays an essential part in communication today. It is fast, immediate and ensures that the same message is received by the maximum number of people at the same time. The secret is to use the most appropriate channel for the message.

Audio-conferencing

This is suitable for a maximum of ten participants and has the benefit of being easy to set up and inexpensive. With a group of more than five participants the process will run more smoothly if a chairperson is appointed who can facilitate the management of the meeting.

Each participant should introduce themselves at the beginning and if there are more than three or four speakers, it is helpful for the listeners if the speaker identifies himself each time before speaking. Enthusiastic participants should restrain themselves and not talk over other speakers. It is possible with an Internet link for participants to share documents and data with each other via their PCs. Remember at the end of the meeting to confirm decisions, actions to be taken and deadlines to be met.

Video-conferencing

As the cost of equipment has decreased, many more organisations are using this technology for regular meetings, often within the same country. These systems can either work point to point between two sites, or multi-site via a video-conferencing service provider.

In theory any number of sites can be involved; however, four sites with three or four participants at each site is the maximum that can work effectively in practice. It is possible to bring in additional people on an audio line. An object or a graphics camera can highlight visual aids or even 3-D objects and PCs can add PowerPoint slides, documents and spreadsheets.

Instruction in the use of video-conferencing tends to focus on the technical detail and there is little or no training on how to present yourself to people halfway round the world. I do not intend to cover the equipment here, but simply to offer a few pointers as to what will add to or detract from the impact you make.

Before the meeting

- Identify the purpose of the meeting and what you and others are seeking to achieve. Make sure all the sites agree on this. Consider who else will be present – their needs, attitude and level of knowledge.

- Brain-storm your ideas and structure the points you need to make.

- Make a list of the key questions you may be asked and prepare answers to them. List questions you would like to ask. Decide whether you need to discuss any points with colleagues prior to the meeting.

- Produce an agenda and distribute it to other meeting attendees at all sites.

- Prepare notes or visuals that you will need for the meeting.

On the day of the meeting

- Tidy the room and desk and remember to keep confidential documents out of the way.

- Ensure that the television screens/camera are correctly positioned and that the camera is not facing sunlight or bright lights. Ceiling lights need to be on unless there is plenty of natural light.

- At least 20 minutes before the meeting go on line and check and familiarise yourself with the equipment.

- Video-conferencing requires the same restrictions on clothes and accessories as appearing on TV. Therefore, try to avoid sparkling jewellery, spectacles that might catch the light, jazzy ties and clothing with plaids and narrow stripes. Also avoid large areas of white, as these can cause glare.

- When everyone is in the room check seating arrangements and enter pre-sets. If there is more than one person at each site a pre-set can include two to three people. Check the pre-sets with the other site, or sites. Each site should note the pre-sets of the other site. You can use the equipment more creatively by setting the camera pre-sets to zoom in on the speaker.

- Nominate someone to operate the control pad and someone to operate the object camera on which you can display your visuals.

- Nominate a chairperson at the master site and a meeting leader at each of the other sites. Then go through a roll call at each location so that participants can introduce themselves. Using the object camera, show your agenda to the other sites.

- You may find it useful for identification purposes to have your site name and participants' names in front of them throughout the conference.

- If you are using a voice-activated camera, two people talking simultaneously can cause rapid video switching, so ensure that the speaker at the on-screen site has finished speaking before you respond. For multi-site calls you can also put your microphone on mute and only become 'live' when you wish to speak.

- Remember, it is totally unnecessary to shout or even raise your voice above the normal conversational level.

- This is the time to practise your best pronunciation. Speak clearly and slowly. This is particularly important if you are talking to those whose mother tongue is different from yours. Be careful not to include technical shorthand or abbreviations that may be incomprehensible to other sites.

• If you are reading from notes vary your tone and pace and look up regularly towards the camera in order to maintain eye contact with the other sites.

• Your posture throughout the meeting is important; try to keep still as body, head and hand movement can cause the image to break up at the other sites. Avoid shuffling paper, coughing or carrying on side conversations that may be picked up by the microphone. Even picking up and putting down your pen or tapping a pencil will be audible and amplified.

• Be concise, avoid waffle and adding extra detail once you have finished your main point. Pause, look for the reaction and, if necessary, invite questions. Wait for a response and then continue or indicate that you are handing over to someone else.

• For private discussions with colleagues suspend the meeting for a short time. Remember to switch your microphone off, and the camera if necessary. For privacy you can also pass a note to a colleague.

Email

This can be used as part of the audio or video-conferencing preparation for arranging dates and times and distributing agendas.

However, it has an added advantage when participants are geographically spread around the globe and in 'non-compatible' time zones. For instance, at midday in London, Tokyo is going to bed and San Francisco is still fast asleep.

Email provides an ideal method of sharing information between people in these cities.

Internet conferencing

You can also use the Internet as an on-line meeting forum; however, it is slow and the least personal method of communicating with a group of people.

Cross-cultural Meetings

Watch your language

Many international companies use English as their corporate language and have local offices around the world. With the speed of travel and the advent of video-conferencing, at some time you will probably find yourself in the situation where your audience's mother tongue is not English.

There are a number of techniques and strategies to make sure that language differences don't affect the impact of your message. How you tackle the situation will depend on various issues:

• the size of the audience;

• how well they understand spoken English;

• the balance of mother tongue to learnt English.

I will first look at what I consider to be the easiest and probably the most common situation – a small group (under twelve people) whose mother tongue is not English, but whose knowledge is good to excellent. You don't need an interpreter, but you should be aware that you can lose your audience in a number of ways:

- Avoid double negatives: 'If we don't invest in this plant now, we won't be able to achieve targets next year.' A clearer construction would be, 'We must invest in this plant now to achieve next year's targets.'

- Be aware of double meanings to the same word. A chief executive emailed his local manager in Brazil 'fire staff with enthusiasm'. Two days later the local manager replied 'I have followed your instruction and made 300 people redundant.'

- Avoid expressions with a national connotation, for example, collecting your P45.

- Avoid all colloquialisms: 'moving the goal-posts', 'making a pig's ear of it' or 'getting egg on your face'.

- Be aware of national sensitivities. Avoid expressions like 'He behaved like a little Hitler.'

- Avoid abbreviations and acronyms that may not travel well, for example, AIDS is SIDA in French and VAT becomes TVA in French and EVA in Spanish.

With small audiences you can always invite them to say if they don't understand a particular word or expression.

Your delivery should be slower and clearer than if you were talking to people with English as their mother tongue. If you have a regional accent you may want to adopt a more received pronunciation, or think about enunciating clearly to avoid misunderstanding. The following illustrates the difficulty a foreigner may experience when listening to a native English speaker. An English manager was asked to bring along his German colleague for a discussion with a Japanese group as they understood the German's English more easily. He was probably speaking what has come to be known as 'offshore English', with simple grammar, straightforward sentence construction and, of course, no colourful colloquialisms.

General advice on using professional language services

When seeking professional help to cope with a multilingual audience, you will meet translators and interpreters. Interpreters work with the spoken word, while translators reproduce your text in writing, working in their mother tongue.

Before making a presentation which is to be interpreted, allow sufficient time for the interpreter to check any technical terms or corporate expressions with no instant, exact translation.

In fact, some words may simply not exist. With the opening up of the Russian continent, it was discovered that no single word existed for 'marketing'. Equally, as women's equality is introduced and discussed in China, new words have to be invented in Mandarin.

It is important for the interpreter to see a transcript of your talk in advance. This avoids any such problems. Failing that, at least try to meet her before your presentation. Remember that she may have questions of her own which will help her to do a competent job for you.

Another area of difficulty is humour. I know of one speaker who was delighted with the reception that his humorous story received at a major conference. It was only later that he learnt that the interpreter had, in fact, said to the audience, 'the speaker is now telling a funny story – will you please laugh'.

Interpretation

There are various styles of interpreting. The ones you are most likely to encounter are simultaneous and consecutive.

Simultaneous interpreting

Simultaneous interpreting describes the situation where the interpreter talks at the same time as you do. This can happen in one of two ways. When the interpreter speaks quietly in the room, seated beside any member of the audience who needs assistance, this is called 'whispering interpreting'. In some situations a manager may understand the language, but be reluctant to ask a question, and would require the services of a whispering interpreter to do so on his behalf, to ensure clarity and intelligibility. If you are presenting in this situation, be aware that there will be somebody speaking in a low voice all the time during your presentation. Regular breaks should be scheduled if only one interpreter is present, as this is a tiring and intensive activity.

Alternatively, at large conferences where many people need to listen to a second language, two interpreters work in relay, seated in a soundproof booth with a large, clear window giving them full view of you and your presentation. In the latter situation, you and members of your audience need to have access to headphones in order to hear the voice of the interpreter. Anyone who speaks in the meeting room must use a microphone, which feeds sound into the booth, otherwise the interpreter cannot hear what is said.

Wherever she is seated, bear in mind that the interpreter may need longer to explain expressions and, although you may speak at a normal rate, you should plan to allow pauses between chunks of information. It is also important to avoid standing in front of a visual aid the interpreter may have to refer to or even translate. In an ideal layout, you should be in visual contact with the interpreter. Any verbal communication would normally be made through the chairperson of the meeting.

If you are to use a microphone to speak or headsets in order to listen to interpreters during a question-and-answer session, it is always advisable to check the settings and ask technicians for advice on how to use them before making your presentation.

Consecutive interpreting

When the interpreter waits until you have finished speaking before repeating what you have said in the other language, this is called 'consecutive interpreting'.

The same issues need to be considered as for simultaneous interpreting. However, in this situation, after expressing each chunk of ideas you will need to wait for the interpreter to finish repeating this, before continuing with your presentation. Again, it is important for the interpreter to have a copy of your script in advance so that any difficulties may be identified and resolved.

Don't forget that if, for any reason, the interpreter is prevented from understanding or following your presentation, you will lose the opportunity to get your message across to part of your audience.

Visual aids

If you are presenting to an international audience you must decide the language of your visual aids. The IT company, Cisco Systems, uses English visual aids, even when presenting in a foreign language. Often the terms are extremely technical and no translation exists. If you face this situation, it is important to explain the terms and possibly add another visual aid for greater clarity. Although, in Chapter 5 How to Design Visual Aids, I stressed my dislike of word slides, when presenting to an international audience I feel they can help to put your message across.

This is particularly true when addressing Japanese audiences who, in general, have a greater command of written English than spoken English. During a meeting in Tokyo a Japanese manager presented me with a sheet of bullet points. He went on to explain each one; however, I was grateful for his notes as his accent was strong which made it difficult to understand him. He was obviously aware of this and had overcome the problem with his bullet point sheet.

If you are responsible for organising a conference or meeting, it is essential that you advise delegates that an inter-pretation service will be available. This will encourage attendance by anyone who may doubt their ability to follow or contribute to proceedings in the main language of the meeting.

Final Words

If in doubt, tackle the problem head-on as one speaker did when addressing a bi-lingual conference. 'It's common for the English to start their presentation with a joke. I am French, but I am speaking in English, so what should I do?' This was, I think, a very acceptable way of building a rapport with both the English and the French members of the audience.

SUMMARY

- Be aware of the limitations of virtual meetings.

- Choose the most appropriate channel.

- Engage a professional language services company, if necessary, for multi-cultural meetings.

21

Final Thoughts

As I write the last few pages of this book, it makes me think
of how you might feel the day after a particularly important
speech. For weeks, maybe even months, it has been on your
mind. Sometimes in the forefront as you grappled with the
right choice of words; sometimes in the background as you
watched a television programme and realised that you
could use an amusing line from a comedy show. Then
suddenly it's over. It took months to prepare and only
moments to deliver. You might think you are like a runner
who prepares for a 100m sprint at the Olympic Games. In
fact speaking is not like that at all. There is no winner in the
speaking game. You may win or lose a contract, but not
entirely on your presentation skills. Rarely is speaking a one-
off event. Developing your ability to speak effectively is a
continuous process.

   Now you've read this book, you will see its basic difficulty:
that you can't learn to speak just by reading. Trying to do so
would be like trying to learn to ride a bike from a book. I've
written about the techniques but that is only a tiny fraction of
effective speaking. Now you are able to identify all the parts of
the bike, you understand the principles of balance and where
you should put your hands and your feet. You know how to

indicate where you're going. Now is the moment to hop on and have a ride.

Reading this book or any other won't make you a good speaker, but practising will. Unfortunately, unlike bike riding, you can't use a quiet back street to learn the basics of speaking. You need an audience to judge its effectiveness. They will be there to see all your attempts to keep your balance and to witness the occasional crash. But crashes are part of the learning process. If you've ever watched a baby learning to walk you'll know that initial failures are inevitable. The trick is not to be discouraged. Imagine a baby saying to itself as it fell back on its bottom for the umpteenth time: 'I'll never get the hang of this. I'm just making a fool of myself, I'll have to give up.' You must keep at it.

Opportunities to Practise

If you feel shy, search out occasions to speak outside work, like to the sixth form at your old school, at the local sports club, or to the residents' association. If you are totally inexperienced set yourself the goal of asking a question at your next meeting. I know speakers who attend public meetings with the sole objective of asking a question. They sit close to the front so that they can't be ignored. As soon as question time is announced, up shoot their hands to 'speak in public'. If you decide to practise like this you will probably find you experience the same symptoms of nervousness as you do when you are giving a talk. Your heart will beat faster and you'll have a dry mouth and sweaty palms. Acknowledge all your feelings; don't try to fight them. Be aware of your physical state, but don't allow it to control you.

In a meeting at work when you have no specific role, ensure that you speak up within the first 10 minutes. The longer you leave it the more difficult it will be to contribute. Simply offer agreement, 'Yes that's true, we've noticed that too' or ask for more information, 'Could you give me an example of how that happened?' Speaking up early will establish your presence and make it easier for you to speak again.

As you become more proficient, consider volunteering to chair a meeting or to give a vote of thanks at your social club. Each occasion will be a challenge and an opportunity to become familiar with your anxiety. Turn it into positive energy to stimulate original thoughts and entertaining ideas.

Enjoyment

If you are an experienced speaker you probably know already how you could become more effective. Maybe there is only one reason why this doesn't happen: lack of time. You know that you should pay more attention to your preparation. You realise you should rehearse. You understand the value of good visual aids but you don't have the time. No one can change that but you. The presentations and talks you give may not be crucial to you and your company, but if you want to improve as a speaker you'll need to make the time for it. Going on courses or reading books won't change you from being a mediocre speaker into an exceptional one. Only you can do that.

Effective speakers find time to prepare and practise, but the most vital part of a good speaker is much more difficult to acquire. It's in their hearts and shines out for everyone to appreciate. It's the magical quality of enjoyment. In other chapters I have stressed enthusiasm, sincerity and vitality. These are all based on the speaker's ability to enjoy communicating with his or her audience. Enjoyment is contagious. The audience will enjoy your talk if you enjoy giving it.

Thank you for being a good listener. I suspect you haven't agreed with everything I've said, but I hope that my suggestions will help you to capture the butterflies and train them to fly in formation.

Further Reading

Philippa Davies, *Total Confidence: The complete guide to self-assurance and personal success*, Piatkus, 1995

Philippa Davies, *Your Total Image*, Piatkus, 1996

Dr Lillian Glass, *Confident Conversation*, Piatkus, 1991

Malcolm Kushner, *Successful Presentations for Dummies: A reference for the rest of us*, IDG Books Worldwide Inc, 1996

Lee Glickstein, *Be Heard Now! Tap into your inner speaker and communicate with ease*, Broadway Books, 2000

Patsy McCarthy and Caroline Hatcher, *Speaking Persuasively: How to make the most of your presentations*, Allen & Unwin, 1996

Brian Roet, *The Confidence to Be Yourself*, Piatkus, 1999

Brian Roet, *Understanding Hypnosis*, Piatkus, 2000

Phyllis Shindler, *100 Best After-Dinner Stories*, Piatkus, 1992

Phyllis Shindler, *My Lords, Ladies and Gentlemen*, Piatkus, 1986

Phyllis Shindler, *Raise Your Glasses*, Piatkus, 1999

Peter Thompson, *Persuading Aristotle: A Masterclass in the timeless art of strategic persuasion in business*, Kogan Page, 1999

Useful Addresses

Voice Development

Roz Comins
Co-ordinator, Voice Care Network UK, 29 Southbank Road,
Kenilworth, Warwickshire CV8 1LA. Tel/Fax: 01926 864000

Meribeth Bunch
Communication Arts & Associates Ltd, 12a Crediton Hill,
London NW6 1HP. Tel: 020 7916 2905
Email: meribethb@aol.com

Samantha Cones
Tel: 020 8870 5008
email: sam_cones@hotmail.com

Rosalind Adler
87 Cedar Grove, London W5 4AT. Tel: 020 8810 0955

Humorist

Martin Nicholls
Albany House, Albany Crescent, Claygate, Esher, Surrey
KT10 0PF. Tel: 01372 468022

Speaking Clubs

D. Carlyle
National Development Officer, Association of Speakers
Clubs, 3 Westfield Avenue, Beverley HU17 7HA.
Tel: 01482 882519

Toastmasters International
Contact: Mike Silverman. Tel: 07071 222 915

Misha Carder
Co-ordinator, Speaking Circles, 76 Lower Oldfield Park,
Oldfield Park, Bath BA2 3HP. Tel: 01225 464333

Scriptwriters

Mark Oglesby
4 Beverley Road, London W4 2LP. Tel: 020 8995 0526
email: markoglesby@compuserve.com

Phillip Khan-Panni
PKP Communications, 35 Hillbrow Road, Bromley, Kent
BR1 4JL. Tel: 020 8466 7026
email: speaks@pkp.co.uk

Equipment Hire

Carpenter Communications Group Limited
45 Holloway Lane, Harmondsworth, West Drayton,
Middlesex UB7 0AE. Tel: 020 8897 2736

Stocks CameraCrew
5 Havyatt, Glastonbury, Somerset BA6 8LF.
Tel: 01749 870071

Presentation Equipment

Universal AV Services Limited
St Annes House, Guy Street, Bradford BD4 7BB.
Tel: 01274 307763. Fax: 01274 390243

Digital Audio Visual Group (The Computing Suppliers Federation)
8 Canalside, Lowersmoor Wharf, Worcester WR1 2RR.
Tel: 01905 727610. Fax: 01905 727619
Email: info@csf.org.uk
Website: www.csf.org.uk

Professional Language Services

Susie Kershaw
SK Associates, 10 Barley Mow Passage, London W4 4PH.
Tel: 020 8994 6477. Fax: 020 8994 9082

Video-conferencing

Alan Tittler
Mar-Com Systems Limited, Mar-Com House, 1 Heathlands,
Heath Gardens, Twickenham, Middlesex TW1 4BP.
Tel: 020 8891 5061

Useful Websites

www.starlingtech.com/quotes
www.quotations.com
www.quoteland.com
www.quotationlocation.com
www.nsaspeaker.org
www.presentations.com
www.toastmasters.org

Media Directories

Willings Press Guide
Hollis Directories Limited, Harlequin House, 7 High Street,
Teddington, Middlesex TW11 8EL. Tel: 020 8943 3138.
Fax: 020 8943 5151
Website: www.willingspressguide.com

PIMS (UK) Limited
PIMS House, Mildmay Avenue, London N1 4RS.
Tel: 020 7354 7000. Fax: 020 7354 7053
Website: www.pims.co.uk

PR Newswire Europe
210 Old Street, London EC1V 9UN. Tel: 020 7490 8111.
Fax: 020 7490 1255
Website: www.prenewswire.co.uk

PR Planner
Chess House, 34 Germain Street, Chesham, Bucks HP5 1SJ.
Tel: 01494 797260. Fax: 01494 797224
Website: www.mediainfo.co.uk

Overseas Contacts in Training and Communication

Patricia (Patsy) McCarthy
Senior Lecturer – Communication, Faculty of Business,
Queensland Univeristy of Technology, 2 George Street, GPO
Box 2434, Brisbane, Queensland 4001, Australia.
Tel: (07) 3864 2131. Fax: (07) 3864 1811
Email: p.mccarthy@qut.edu.au

Marilyn Wheeler
President, Marilyn Wheeler & Associates Inc, Direct Effect
Programme, 5318 E 2nd Street, #320, Long Beach, California
9080-5354, USA. Tel: (562) 987 1237. Fax: (562) 987 5545
Email: marilyn@mwheeler.com

Index